THE CELTIC AND
SCANDINAVIAN RELIGIONS

HUTCHINSON'S UNIVERSITY LIBRARY

WORLD RELIGIONS

EDITOR:

REV. PROFESSOR E. O. JAMES

M.A., D.LITT., PH.D., D.D., F.S.A.
*Professor of the Philosophy of Religion
in the University of London*

THE CELTIC AND
SCANDINAVIAN RELIGIONS

by

J. A. MacCULLOCH, D.D.

HON. CANON OF THE CATHEDRAL
OF THE HOLY SPIRIT, CUMBRAE

GREENWOOD PRESS, PUBLISHERS
WESTPORT, CONNECTICUT

The Library of Congress has catalogued this publication as follows:

Library of Congress Cataloging in Publication Data

MacCulloch, John Arnott, 1868-1950.
    The Celtic and Scandinavian religions.

    Reprint of the 1948 ed., which was issued as v. 10
of Hutchinson's university library: World religions.
    Bibliography: p.
    1. Celts--Religion. 2. Scandinavia--Religion.
I. Title.
BL900.M38 1973   299'.16   72-11739
ISBN 0-8371-6705-1

NOTE

I HAVE to acknowledge with thanks permission given by Sir Thomas Clark, of the firm of Messrs. T. and T. Clark, to use my earlier book, *The Religion of the Ancient Celts*, and my Celtic articles in Dr. Hastings' *Encyclopaedia of Religion and Ethics*, both published by that firm, to the representatives of the late Dr. Hastings for similar permission; and to the Macmillan Co., New York, for their permission to use my *Celtic Mythology* and *Eddic Mythology* in "The Mythology of all Races" series, of which they are the owners.

Originally published in 1948 by Hutchinson.'s University Library, London, New York

Reprinted with the permission of Hutchinson & Co., Publishers, Ltd.

Reprinted in 1973 by Greenwood Press, Inc.,
51 Riverside Avenue, Westport, Conn. 06880

Library of Congress catalog card number 72-11739

ISBN 0-8371-6705-1

Printed in the United States of America

10 9 8 7 6 5 4 3 2

CONTENTS

PREFACE

THIS book, like the rest of those in the Series, is intended both for the general reader and for the student. The general reader will find in it enough to satisfy his intellectual curiosity regarding what and how the Celtic people thought and worshipped, including those who lived in Britain before and after the Roman conquest. It is also intended to give the general reader some account of the religious beliefs and practices of the Scandinavians, many of whom, as Vikings or Northmen, raided our shores and held sway in parts of Britain for several centuries.

Students who wish to have a general survey of Celtic and Scandinavian religions before passing on to more detailed study, will find, I hope, the book sufficient to satisfy their immediate needs. In the Scandinavian section it will, as I trust, serve as an introduction to the Old Norse texts.

J. A. MacCulloch

Edinburgh,
1948.

CELTIC

CHAPTER I

THE CELTIC PEOPLE

FROM early times the Celts had occupied considerable parts of Central Europe, between the upper parts of the rivers Danube, Rhine, and Elbe. They spread thence and occupied the valley of the Po and other parts of Northern Italy, in the later parts of the sixth century B.C. Much later, about 390 B.C., they were able to advance as far as Rome, which they raided, the Capitol alone escaping. Eventually the Celtic region in North Italy was conquered by the Romans. In 279 B.C. some of the Celts had advanced into Greece and pillaged Delphi, Galatia was also occupied by them. In the west the Celts penetrated into Gaul and parts of Spain, Ireland and Britain were also occupied, the latter by several groups of invaders. Thus their empire, if this name may be fittingly applied to the wide region which they occupied, stretched across Europe from east to west.

The word Gaul was used comprehensively for two regions— Cisalpine Gaul, which meant the Celtic-occupied territory in Northern Italy south of the Alps, and Transalpine Gaul, part of Switzerland, part of Germany, Belgium, and France.

Of this, Celtic Gaul, more truly Celtic, stretched from the Loire to the Seine and Marne. North-east of this was Belgic Gaul, less purely Celtic; to the south-east was Aquitania. Cæsar conquered Gaul about the middle of the first century B.C., and thenceforth it became a Roman province.

The Celts, during the time of their empire, are not to be regarded as a homogeneous people, under one sovereign. Their empire was never compact as the Roman Empire became. There was a legendary King, Ambicatus, who was said to have ruled over a large part of the Celtic area, but he belongs rather to fiction than to fact. What was most likely was the dominance of one or more strong tribes over the others. In

Gaul, in Cæsar's time, we see something of this kind—a supremacy or attempted supremacy of one tribe over the others. For this supremacy the Arverni disputed with the Aedui. From the second century B.C. to the beginning of the Christian era the far-spread lands occupied by the Celts had become part of the Roman Empire, except Ireland and northern Scotland.

The Celts, especially as they spread far and wide, were not a pure race. They mixed with those peoples whom they conquered, thoroughly Celticizing them. Their real unity was a unity of language and of religious beliefs. There was no one racial or anthropological type common to all, but Celtic speech was imposed and accepted wherever they conquered.

Cæsar, having conquered Gaul, invaded Britain, but only later Roman conquest, beginning with the invasion of Claudius, A.D. 43-47, made Britain a Roman province, extending in the north to the area between Forth and Clyde, where Antonine's wall was erected against the unconquered tribes to the north. Then in the reign of Commodus (A.D. 180-192) and in the immediately succeeding years the Romans made their northern frontier in Britain the line of Hadrian's wall, begun c. A.D. 130. Henceforth, the tribes south of that became, like those of Gaul, Romanized.

How early the successive waves of Celtic invasion reached Britain is uncertain. The first may have come in the Bronze Age, and perhaps were the Celtic group, known as Goidels, speaking the Gadhelic or Gaelic branch of Celtic speech. Here it should be noted that in Celtic speech there had developed a phonetic difference, which had perhaps already existed on the continent before the invasions of the British Isles began. It is characterized by the change of qu by certain groups into p. The Goidels retained qu, later c or k; others—the Gauls and the Brythons, as the p-using Celtic groups in Britain came to be called, made the change into p. Thus each or ech, "horse," in Gadhelic, is in Brythonic epos. Again maqvi, later mac, is in Welsh map or with p changed to b, mab, or with the m dropped ap or ab. Gadhelic speech is now represented in Irish and Scots Gaelic and in Manx. Brythonic speech survived in Welsh, Cornish (now extinct), and Breton. This p was used also by the Gauls. The Romans never penetrated into Ireland, nor, apparently, did any of the Brythonic Celts.

The Goidels formed the first wave of Celtic invaders from the continent. Did they occupy Britain or did they make their first landing in Ireland? This question has been much debated, some holding that they first came to Britain, where, at a later time, they were conquered by Brythonic invaders; others that they never entered Britain, but went to Ireland, perhaps from Spain, as Irish tradition in the annals attests, and eventually came, as the Scots from Ireland, to Argyllshire (Dalriada), towards the end of the fifth century. For the purpose of our investigation into Celtic religion the question is immaterial.

The later waves of Brythonic invasion brought with them in the early Iron Age, the Halstatt culture, so-called from discoveries made at Halstatt in Austria in 1846. This culture shows the transition from the Bronze to the Iron Age. Then in the Iron Age came the La Tène or Marnian culture (500 B.C. to the Christian era), these names coming from the great finds at La Tène in Switzerland, and in the valley of the Marne in France. The objects which characterize the Halstatt and La Tène cultures are of varying kinds—arms, shields, bridles, brooches, mirrors, situlae, and many others. These, especially in the La Tène period, are well made and well proportioned, they are beautifully ornamented in different designs. There is a use of coral for decoration and also of enamel. Both craftsmen and artists showed wonderful gifts of handicraft and of pleasing decoration, which have not often been exceeded.

The final invasions before the Romans arrived were those of the Belgae (about 75 B.C., and in 50 B.C.), people with some Teutonic admixture, but speaking Celtic. The region which they occupied first was the south-east and south of England. They were an active conquering people, who practised agriculture in the valleys rather than on the uplands, as their predecessors had done. They cut down forests, cleared them for fields, using a wheeled plough drawn by oxen for turning over the soil. Early in Cæsar's invasion the other tribal rulers had made Cassivellaunus supreme ruler, though he, as head of the

Catuvellauni, had been aggressive to them. He opposed Cæsar, but had to capitulate to him.

We need not assume that the Celts in Britain, any more than those in Gaul, were savages, Cæsar's woad-dyed and skin-clad folk, though tribes further north, away from continental influence, would be less advanced. They were barbaric, but some of them had attained a fair degree of civilization. They were farmers, hunters, craftsmen—potters, weavers, metal-workers, traders, warriors. Some had ships, perhaps not so well-built as the large, oaken vessels of the Veneti of Brittany, which caused trouble to Cæsar and in which they carried on trade with Britain. These vessels were two hundred and twenty in number when Cæsar encountered them.

The artistic work of the Celts, as shown by the Hallstatt and La Tène objects found in Gaul and Britain, was skilful and beautiful. Many of the tribes had a coinage, specimens of which have survived in large numbers. The La Tène people introduced the chariot, the force of which in battle Cæsar describes and which caused amazed terror among his troops, just as the first employment of tanks in the first great war did. They were driven down upon the enemy, confusing their ranks. The occupants jumped down from them and fought on foot. The charioteers drove back to the rear, so that their owners, if hard pressed, might retreat. Thus, says Cæsar, they had both the mobility of cavalry and the stability of infantry.

By the beginning of the Christian era the Celtic regions on the continent had become part of the Roman Empire. Southern Britain was conquered by the Romans in the first century A.D.

CHAPTER II

ASPECTS OF NATURE WORSHIP

THE earliest Celtic worship, like that of most other peoples, was given to spirits of nature, of the sea, rivers, trees, mountains, sky, and heavenly bodies, some of which, as time went on, became more personal deities. All parts of nature were alive, as man was, and he found these friendly or hostile. At a later time worshipful deities might be connected with this or that part of nature. The belief in animism, the belief that everything was alive, tenanted by a soul or spirit, has been universal. As man's spirit might leave him, temporarily in sleep or, finally, at death, so the spirits of natural objects might be separated from these. The spirit of a tree might leave the tree and become more or less independent of it, the god of the tree. But as, in a forest, there are many trees, so there rose in man's imagination many tree-spirits, which might resolve themselves into groups of beings, now kindly, now dangerous, to man. Where there was but one object of its kind—sun, moon, earth, sea—the spirit of each would tend to become a being more or less separate from it, yet still ruling it or connected with it, a sun, moon, earth, or sea deity. Thus in time, besides the greater gods of nature, there would be also groups of nature spirits, connected with rivers, forests, mountains, and other parts of nature. The worship of these continued long after more personal deities were evolved and worshipped, and in one form or another continued among the peasantry even after the coming of Christianity. Gildas (sixth century) said that "the blind people" paid divine honours to mountains, hills, springs, rivers, i.e., to the spirits of these. The Celtic people were not alone in paying such divine honours to parts of nature: it is a form of worship which is of great antiquity.

It is possible that the earth was regarded as female, and that earth and under-earth were held to be one. Earth was the source of fertility and important to all who depended much on agriculture. The earth mother or earth goddess was eventually replaced by an earth-god, with her as his consort. But locally her position may have remained prominent. The Matres, with their widespread worship, their symbols—cornucopia, fruit, flowers—showing their connection with fertility, were three in number, triple forms of an earlier earth-goddess, in accordance with a Celtic tendency to triplicate a deity. These will be considered later, as well as the prominence of goddesses in Irish belief, as mothers of divine groups, with outstanding functions even where gods with similar functions existed.

Mountains and hills were venerated for themselves, or as abodes of deities, as later inscriptions show, e.g., one "To the mountains," and worship was offered on heights. Vosegus was deity of the Vosges mountains, Arduinna of the wooded heights of the Ardennes, Abnoba of those of the Black Forest, or of these divinized.

Forests, woods, and trees were worshipped. A god named Silvanus, the Roman sylvan deity, is mentioned in many inscriptions, though these do not give the native name. The Fatae Dervones or Matronae Dervones were spirits or goddesses of oak-woods. Claudian speaks of the sacred oaks of the Hercynian forest, and Pliny's words are significant. "The Druids hold nothing more sacred than the mistletoe and the tree on which it grows, provided that it be an oak. They seek the oak for their sacred groves, and no ceremony is complete without its branches. Whatever grows on the tree is sent from heaven, a sign of the choice of the tree by the god himself." Maximus of Tyre speaks of the Celts revering a great oak as Zeus, though he does not give the native name of the deity. In the Pyrenean district a group of six trees was sacred to a god, and elsewhere groves were regarded as highly sacred places. In Ireland certain trees, oak or ash, called *bile*, were regarded with reverence, sometimes growing over a sacred well, and they must not be cut down. One was described as "a firm, strong god"; the destruction of another by a hostile tribe was regarded with horror. Myth spoke of the wonderful trees of the divine land, and of such trees having accidentally been planted on earth and then carefully guarded. Trees were perhaps first regarded as embodying the spirit of vegetation, then as sacred to a deity, or if a tree grew on a burial mound, it would be thought to embody the spirit of the dead. In Celtic festivals a tree as the abode of the spirit of vegetation was carried in procession to confer benefit on the fields. A tree growing beside a sacred well was also sacred. Up to quite recent times on such a tree was hung a rag or article of clothing belonging to the person who looked for healing from the well. It is the medium through which disease passes to the tree, or healing power from well or tree to the sufferer, or it may be an attenuated form of an earlier offering. Such customs thus surviving indicate what the earlier beliefs had been.

Waters—rivers, lakes, wells—were sacred, themselves divine or the abode of a spirit or deity. Celtic words like *deivos*, *deva*, *dianna*, *diona*, meaning "divine" or "brilliant," were applied to rivers on the continent and in Britain—Dee, Devon, Divona (near Bordeaux), Divonne (in Ain), and others, showing that many rivers were regarded as divine or the home of a spirit or goddess, less often a god. Other rivers with different names were also personified as deities, e.g., *dea Icauna* (the Yonne), *deus Nemausus* (Nimes). Rivers were sources of fertility as well as of other gifts: hence they were venerated and offerings were made to them. But it should be noted that other beings, monstrous and harmful, dwelt in rivers or lakes, water-horses, water-bulls, and the like, and these have survived in popular lore and legend.

Equally divine were many springs and wells, especially those which had medicinal properties. There were spirits and gods or goddesses of such springs, as we shall see. All such were the objects of popular worship. The goddesses or spirits of such places were regarded as beautiful, and their personality was deeply impressed on the people. Long after Christianity prevailed they were still remembered and some sort of devotion paid to them, as there was to trees. They reappeared also as fays or fairies in the Romances and in folk-tales. In the earlier cult, as in the later superstitious devotion, offerings were made to them. Models of limbs had been presented in shrines of healing-spirits or deities, in the hope that healing would come to the donors. Leaden tablets were placed in wells, with inscriptions showing that the wells were personified or inhabited by a spirit or a more personal deity, and the desire of better health is expressed on them. At Amélie-les-Bains the spirits of the well were called Niskai.

In later days fish or eels in such springs were regarded as sacred and must not be destroyed. At an earlier time these would be thought to embody the spirit of the well. Sacred wells exist all over the Celtic area, as indeed elsewhere. They are named after a saint, which doubtless means that he had succeeded to the spirit or deity of the well, often by some action of his own there. Adamnan, in his Life of St. Columba, tells how the saint came to a well, worshipped as a deity, or as the place of spirits. By his act the spirits (demons) fled from it and never returned. It was now believed to cure diseases because the saint had blessed it. The later customs for healing at sacred wells probably were derived from those of pagan times. The patient passed thrice round the well sun-wise in silence, besought the saint for healing, drank the water or washed the diseased limb with it. An offering was made or some part of his clothing placed on the sacred tree which usually overhung the well. "Sun-wise" (in Irish Gaelic *deisiul*) had an important place in Celtic belief and custom. At festivals in Gaul liquor circulated thus, and in Ireland to this sun-wise direction much attention was paid.

The spirits of waters were not all beneficent. Nature is both kindly and hostile; its wilder recesses were apt to be more sinister than other parts of it. Hence man was liable to people not only waters but forests and mountains with uncouth and dangerous beings. This was not confined to the Celts, for it is found everywhere and has given rise to much folk-lore.

Sea-gods, Manannan, Ler, Dylan, will be discussed later. Meanwhile we note that the sea itself was personified, but that it and its waves were regarded as hostile to man, and they were attacked with weapons by Celtic warriors, both on the continent and in Ireland. But the sea had also a more kindly aspect, its waves moaning for the deaths of men, or their sound having prophetic aspects.

How far the moon and the sun were worshipped is not certain, though in Ireland there is some evidence for moon worship, and in Gaul there are a few inscriptions which mention sun and moon, while some goddesses equated with Diana may have been connected with the moon. One inscription speaks of the genius of the sun and the moon. It is possible that the moon was regarded with greater awe than the sun as a living object. The moon was the measure of time, and nights preceded days, but attempts were made to synchronize the lunar and solar years over a period of five years, as the calendar found at Coligny, near Lyons, shows. The quinquennial sacrifices spoken of by Diodorus Siculus may have been offered at the beginning of each five-year period. In Ireland oaths were taken by various parts of nature, including the moon, and the breaker of an oath was punished by these. Processes of agriculture were begun with a waxing moon, to promote growth. In some regions there is evidence for festivals occurring at the time of the new moon.

The sacred fires at Celtic festivals—Beltane, Midsummer, both represented the powers of the sun or sun-god and helped to strengthen those. The god Belenos, whose worship was widespread in Gaul, possibly also in Britain, was identified with Apollo. Images found in Gaul of a nameless god with a wheel, a frequent symbol of the sun, may be those of a sun-god, just as numerous model wheels in various metals, found in many places, may be symbols of the sun, as may also be the swastika and triskele, appearing on monuments in Gaul. In Ireland St. Patrick spoke of the worship of the sun.

In Irish tales and in the annalistic account of the invasions of Ireland there are preserved charms which show how different parts of the land were personified and addressed. This, besides the oaths taken by the parts of nature, and such words as those of the War-goddess, Morrigan, telling the mountains, the waters, the rivers, of the victory of the Tuatha Dé Danann, are significant of the personification of different parts of nature and of their divine aspect.

The worship of animals, giving rise later to divinities with animal form or attributes, has been universal, and it is found among the Celts. The boar appears on ensigns and is found on coins and as an image. A statue of Diana riding a wild boar suggests that a native goddess had become the anthropomorphic form of the animal, which now appears as the symbol of the goddess. The swine must have been worshipped, and from it was evolved a god Moccus, a name which means "swine," and this god is identified with Mercury in some inscriptions. Various tales or myths in Ireland and in Wales refer to monstrous or magic swine, and may point to a former cult of the animal.

The bear was also a sacred animal, its name *artos* occurs in place-names like Arto-dunum, Artobranos, and in personal names—Artogenos (Arthgen), "son of the bear," pointing to the belief that the bear or bear-god might be father of a son. A goddess Artio is mentioned, and a god Artaios was equated with Mercury, though it is uncertain whether his name is derived from *artos* or connected with *ar*, "ploughed land." There was a goddess Andarta, the first part of the name *and* being augmentative. These may be compared with the Greek Artemis Brauronia, Artemis as a Bear-goddess. The numerous place-names in Gaul which have *artos* as part of the name may belong to local sites of a bear cult. They are nearly two hundred in all.

The bull was another divine animal and is represented on a monument from Paris, that which is usually described as "the bull with the three cranes," from the presence of these birds upon it. The name on the monument is Tarvos (from *taruos*, *tarvos*, "bull"). Trigaranos ("three cranes") and on other sides the god Esus is depicted cutting down a tree, the branches of which extend over the bull. On an altar fragment from Tréves is shown a male figure (Esus?) cutting down a tree, in the branches of which a bull's head and three cranes appear. Some myth is depicted, but in spite of attempts to connect what appears on these monuments with incidents in Irish mythology, its significance is unknown. Bulls appear on coins or are engraved on stone or have been found as statuettes, and these occur in England and in the north of Scotland, and in the centre and east of Gaul. As represented the bull is sometimes three-horned. The name *tarvos* appears in many names of tribes, personal and place-names, all showing the wide extent of this bull worship.

A worship of the horse existed, and the horse appears as a symbol on many coins. A large image of a stallion was found at Neuvy-en-Sullias. It bears a dedication to a god Rudiobus, but whether the animal represents this god is unknown. This formed part of a large hoard, perhaps hidden by pagans when Christianity prevailed in Gaul. For the most part the worship of the horse was superseded over a large area by that of a horse-goddess, Epona (p. 30). A mule god, Mullo, equated with Mars, is known from several inscriptions.

As in many other parts of the world the serpent was worshipped. In representations of the reptile it is horned, the horn being often a symbol of divinity, or it has a ram's head; it appears with other Celtic deities who hold serpents or present a torque to ram's-headed serpents. The serpent was connected with the underworld, and it is sometimes depicted with a horned god, who may be Cernunnos, the underworld deity. The ram was associated with the worship of the dead, and small statuettes of it have been found in tombs in Gaul. Giving the serpent, an underworld animal, a ram's head, may have been thought appropriate. Such ram's-headed serpents appear on monuments alone or beside a deity, usually the crouching god, sometimes a three-headed deity. One of them is also associated with a Gaulish Mercury.

When a worshipful animal became anthropomorphic, the resultant deity might be represented with some part of the animal, e.g., the head. This might also appear in myths about the deity. Thus horned deities, of whom Cernunnos is one, represent the animal deities from which they had been evolved, Cernunnos from some kind of stag. Sometimes an animal has three horns, as if to emphasize its divinity or its divine strength. The cult of divine animals accounts for their appearance on standards carried into battle, a custom which the Celts shared with other peoples, opposing their foes with their worshipful animals. Similarly they were represented on helmets, as if taking the wearers under their protection.

The cult or sacredness of animals is associated with totemism, that widespread social arrangement in which a clan is believed to be related to an animal or even a plant, holds every such animal or plant as sacrosanct, never kills or eats it, and considers that there is a mystic bond between members of the clan and members of the animal or plant group. Whether totemism existed among the Celts is an open question, all that can be said is that it might be compatible with certain facts which emerge regarding the sacredness of animals and their cult. Certain groups of persons bear names which point to descent from an animal. There is found a taboo against eating certain animals. Cæsar says that some of the British tribes thought it unlawful to eat the hare, the fowl, and the goose, though they kept them for pastime or pleasure. The first part of his statement is more important than the second, in which he may be speaking in error. Other examples of this are found in survivals, and in myths there are statements which show the ill-luck or worse which followed the eating or killing of an animal with which the eater or killer was somehow associated. Exogamy is another aspect of totemism, a man must marry outside his clan, counting descent through the mother is another. Succession through a sister's son counted for more than direct succession. Facts like these mainly concerned royal houses, e.g., the Pictish, where they may have been survivals, but their occurrence in myths is significant. In heroic or divine groups a hero or a deity is called son of the mother, not of the father, and a prominent position is given among the deities to goddesses.

A custom celebrated on the Kalends of January, of men going about clad in the skins of animals or wearing their masks, survived long enough into Christian times to be condemned. It points to some kind of kinship with sacred animals or of the worshippers' union with them.

CHAPTER III

MYTHIC ASPECTS

As the myths about the gods in Gaul were never written down but only transmitted orally, they did not survive the transformation of the native religion into a Gallo-Roman type. It was different in Ireland where the Romans never penetrated and where, fortunately, even as paganism was passing away or after its passing, there were those sufficiently interested and, if they were Christian, tolerant enough to preserve myths and the like in writing. Some of these have kept their original form; in others the deities have become more or less human, kings and queens, or what is told of them is transmuted into a false historical and annalistic scheme. But from these writings we are able to see what the gods were conceived to be, their powers, their relation to men.

Britain came under the rule of the Romans, and the same transformation of the native religion into a Romano-British scheme at last came about. In Wales, however, there seem to have been preserved certain myths about deities, which became much altered. Here, again, they appear more as kings, queens, heroes, than as deities, and the tales are full of their magic powers. They are regarded as mortal, yet their powers are much more than those of mortals, and it is these which form the turning-point of many of the episodes recorded. Such tales are contained in *The Mabinogion*, and are "nothing more nor less than degraded and adulterated mythological tales" (Ivor B. John, *The Mabinogion*, p. 7). The Irish tales which survive in such large numbers may also be so regarded, but not to such an extent, for in some at least gods and goddesses appear in their divine forms. They are easily seen to be more than mortal, "not troubled by pain and distress," as one of them said. Yet even in the Welsh tales there is sufficient to give some idea of the old pagan beliefs, for as Matthew Arnold said in his *Study of Celtic Literature*, "the medieval story-teller is pillaging an antiquity of which he does not fully possess the secret."

We now turn to some of the mythical conceptions of the deities. Gods sometimes had love affairs with mortals, and this is the theme of many mythical tales in Ireland. Children born of these are objects of their care, and they help them in time of need. The hero Cúchulainn was son of the god Lug, according to one account of him, and when he was fighting against great odds, Lug invisibly attacked his foes. Lug is described as a warrior, tall and fair, with shield, five-pointed spear, and javelin. Moreover he sang a charm over his wounded son, so that he slept, and he cured his wounds with medicinal herbs. The god Manannan was father of Mongan, of whom many strange things are told. Diarmaid, one of the heroes of the Fionn saga, was specially helped by the god Oengus, who invisibly aided him, even causing his enemies to assume one by one the hero's form, so that they were slain by their own friends.

It is not impossible that the first holders of names ending in *genos*, "born of," with the name of a deity preceding it, were believed to be the son of that deity by a mortal mother, e.g. Esugenos, "born of Esus," Camulogenos, "born of Camulos," Totatigenos, "born of Totatis," and others. Similar names suggest descent from an animal or a nature deity, e.g., Artogenos, "son of the bear" (*artos*, "bear"), Dubrogenos, "son of the river" (*dubra*, "waters").

The deities were or were supposed to be by their worshippers, sometimes hostile to men. This usually was from some particular cause, e.g., scorning the amorous approach of a goddess, as when the hero Cúchulainn refused himself to the goddess Morrigan, and she became his enemy. This belief in divine hostility lies behind the offering of propitiatory sacrifices. The gods had been offended by human neglect— particular wrongdoing, the breaking of a taboo, and this was borne witness to by calamities—plague, defeat in war. Hence they must be propitiated and made friendly again by sacrifice. We shall see this exemplified when considering the sacrifices offered by the Celts.

According to Cæsar the Druids discussed and taught many

things concerning the might and power of the immortal gods. They were naturally immortal, yet in Irish story, as in Scandinavian myth, their immortality might depend upon the eating or drinking of some particular food or drink which possessed immortal virtues. Whether this was said of the deities of Gaul is unknown.

The deities had bodily forms, more splendid than those of mortals, and sometimes they appear to be of vast size. Or they assumed the form of animals, e.g. Badb, one of the Irish War-goddesses, that of a crow. Ordinarily they were invisible, "we behold and are not beheld," said one of them, but sometimes they would appear in their divine form, as Bran saw Manannan, god of the sea, crossing the waves in his chariot. When Lug appeared his face had a splendour like that of the setting sun. Sometimes deities appeared as ordinary mortals, even assuming the form of a particular person for their own purposes, or they were seen in different disguises. These things were doubtless true also of the deities of Gaul.

The dwelling of the gods does not appear to have been in a remote heaven, but as we shall see in studying the beliefs about a Celtic Wonderland or divine land, they might dwell in a hill or underground, or on distant islands, or even beneath the sea. But wherever it was situated, it was a desirable place, beautiful, free from toil and trouble, and happy were the mortals who in life were invited thither.

CHAPTER IV

THE DEITIES IN GAUL

THE Celtic people of Gaul and of Britain, south of Hadrian's wall, were conquered by the Romans, and in Britain the Roman rule lasted for over four centuries. The Roman conquest produced in Gaul and Britain a real assimilation to all that was Roman. The Celts, especially in Gaul, had many deities, but most of these were merely local, gods of different tribes, with different names, though with similar functions. Some of these deities, however, were common to several tribes. Over three hundred names of such local deities are known to have existed, most of these in Gaul, some in Britain. The Roman conquerors, knowing of these various divinities, equated them with some of their own deities. Hence Cæsar could speak of the Gauls as worshipping Mercury, Apollo, Mars, Jupiter, Dis, and Minerva. As time went on, and as the Celts submitted to Roman civilization, they accepted these equations. They allowed or even encouraged the Romanizing of their religion as far as the deities and worship were concerned. Indeed, in their growing desire for oneness with Rome, the Gauls tried hard to find as many links as possible, however slight, between their deities and those of Rome. Doubtless some of these equations or assimilations were vague, even haphazard. It could not be expected, e.g., to find complete likeness between a Gaulish deity and Apollo. Thus the Gaulish god Grannos, equated with Apollo, was a god of healing, and, among his many functions, Apollo was a healer, so Grannos was called Apollo-Grannos, regardless of the fact that Apollo had other functions, unknown to Grannos. So with other identifications. The Romans themselves started these assimilations. The Gauls, in their progressive Romanization, now began to build temples, to raise altars, to fashion images of their deities, in the Roman manner, and to have votive inscriptions carved, in which the names of some Roman deities were prefixed or affixed to those of native gods and goddesses. The same was true of other accessories of worship. Thus there came into existence what might be called a Gallo-Roman religion. The same was true of the Celtic tribes in Britain. That there was a thorough Romanization is evident from the statement of the Emperor Claudius, when the Gauls sought representation in the Senate, that they now shared with the Romans in manners, in the arts, and in relationships.

One could hardly say that the gods of Gaul existed as a pantheon. Rather were certain of them deities of a tribe or of a locality, with different names, though the acknowledgment of some local deities may have spread outwards, or the worship of these gods may have been carried to a distance by tribal movements. While it has been thought that three Gaulish gods, Esus, Teutates, and Taranis, whose cruel cult was described by the poet Lucan, were worshipped over a wide area, they were actually no more than local deities. This is shown by the few inscriptions on which their names are found—Esus two, Teutates six, Taranis one. Nor are they found named together on any inscription.

There are many local deities to whom a Roman name has been added, giving several Apollos, Mars, Mercuries. On the other hand some hundreds of local deities, not equated with Roman deities, are named on inscriptions. Their nature and functions are uncertain, or possibly to be discovered through philology.

We turn now to Cæsar's account of the deities of Gaul. He begins with Mercury, who is especially worshipped. Of him there are many images (*simulacra*). He is said to be the inventor of all arts, the ruler of roads and journeys, and he is considered influential in money-making and mercantile affairs. Then came Apollo, Mars, Jupiter, and Minerva, of whom they hold much the same opinion as other races. Apollo drives away disease. Minerva gives the first beginnings of arts and handicrafts. Jupiter holds the heavenly governance. Mars rules over wars. Cæsar adds Dispater, from whom the Gauls say that they are all descended, a belief handed down by the Druids.

To take these in order, there are some nineteen Celtic deities equated with Apollo on inscriptions, giving such combinations as Apollo Grannos, Apollo Belenos, Apollo Maponus. Other deities joined with him are Bormo, Borvo,

Mogounos. The Roman Apollo had several functions, and if a local deity had one of these he was regarded as a Celtic Apollo. Thus the Gaulish Bormo, Borvo, Bormanus, from *bormo*, "warm," was a deity of hot springs, as at Aix-les-bains, Bourbonne-les-bains, and other places, and thus a healer through these, as was Apollo. Grannos seems to have had similar functions, and the Emperor Caracalla is said to have worshipped him along with Æsculapius. Grannos is associated with a native goddess Dirona or Sirona, as Bormo is with Damona, both goddesses of healing. Maponos, which means "a youth," was worshipped by the Brigantes in Britain, and some inscriptions from their territory in north-eastern England exist. He was equated with Apollo regarded as a youthful deity, and is perhaps connected with the Mabon of an old Welsh story, *Kulwych and Olwen* (p. 37). Belenos, whose name means "shining," "resplendent," was known in Cisalpine Gaul and beyond it, and is spoken of by Herodian, Tertullian, and others. He was possibly equated with Apollo as god of light. He may be the Belinus who will be referred to later in considering British divinities.

The Roman god of war, Mars, is equated with some fifty native deities of war in Gaul and also in Britain, the number pointing to the warlike nature of the Celts and to their tribal hostilities. Cæsar speaks of war being a common incident among the tribes, attacking each other or repelling attacks. They were ever ready to pick quarrels. Mars Mullo, known from inscriptions in the north-east of France, and Mars Braciaca, in a British inscription, are less easy to explain. Mullo means "mule," and there may be some reference here to an animal deity, or to some god who attended to traffic. Braciaca means "malt" and the Celts were much given to drink a native brew, but the connexion with Mars is far from clear. Some names of deities assimilated to Mars are interesting, Belatucadros, "comely in slaughter," known from some inscriptions in Britain; Caturix, "battle-chief"; Rigisamus, also known in Britain, "royal" or "kingly."

Of the twenty-five local deities equated with Jupiter in inscriptions, each seldom more than once, few suggest important deities. Some point to local mountain-spirits or gods. Of these the most striking is Pœninus, the deity of the Pennine Alps, where there was a Mons Jovis, and Jupiter Pœninus is named in several inscriptions. Taranos, which may be connected philologically with the German thunder-deity Donar, and Taranucos, are mentioned in a few inscriptions. There are unnamed representations of a god with a wheel or a thunder-bolt, the wheel being a widespread symbol of the sun, which may point to their being native Jupiters. Whether the Gauls regarded them as ruling the sky is far from certain.

At least thirty deities are equated with Mercury in his various functions as a god of speech, or of roads and boundaries, which were important for mercantile enterprise, or of culture generally. This agrees with what Cæsar says of him as inventor of arts, watching over travellers, patron of commerce. Whether he is equally right in regarding the native Mercury as chief god is not so certain. It was said of the Irish god Lug that he possessèd many arts, which corresponds to what Cæsar writes of the native Mercury (p. 25). To the name Mercury on inscriptions is sometimes attached an epithet—*compitalis*, "of the cross-roads," *viator*, "wayfarer," *cultor*, "husbandman," *negotiator* or *mercator*, "trader," *potens lucrorum*, "powerful for gain," pointing to most of the matters over which the Celtic Mercuries ruled. But some of the local deities equated with him do not, by their names, suggest a reason for the equation, e.g., Moccus, a swine-god. On the other hand Cimiacinus, with whom he is equated, is a local god of wayfarers; Arvernus connects him as a tribal god with the Arverni, the great tribe of Auvergne, as does Arvernorix, "King of the Arverni," while Dumiatis links him with the Puy-de-dôme (*dumium*, "summit"), the mountain in that district, on the summit of which was erected a great temple.

Minerva, who teaches the elements of industry and the arts, is represented by a few native goddesses equated with her. One is Cabardiacensis, otherwise unknown, Belisama, and Sul. Belisama is known from two inscriptions, but this is the native name of the Mersey, according to Ptolemy. Sul, whose name is connected with words meaning "burning," "shining," is known mainly in Britain, at Báth, in connexion with the hot springs there, and in whose temple, according to Solinus, perpetual fires burned. She is the equivalent of the Irish culture-goddess Brigit (p. 42).

Cæsar completes his brief survey of Gaulish deities with the statement that the Gauls believe themselves descended from Dispater (the Roman god of the underworld). Hence they determine periods of time by nights, not days. In the beginnings of months and years day follows night. This was part of Druidic teaching, but no myth on the subject has survived. But it may be regarded as originating in a belief, such as is found in many parts of the world, that men had ascended to earth's surface from an underworld region. The native Dis may have been an Earth-god, possibly replacing an earlier Earth-goddess, producing fertility. The native names of this god do not appear on inscriptions conjoined with Dis, but conjecture has been busy in regarding certain images of deities as those of the Gaulish under-world god. One is called Cernunnos (from *cernu*, "horn"), though not all images of a horned god are named. This horned god is sometimes three-headed, and his symbols are those of fertility, appropriate to an earth or underworld deity. Other gods without name are horned, and may be also images of Cernunnos. As in most examples of horned gods elsewhere, the horns symbolize strength, but they may be a relic of an earlier animal-god who had, save for the horns, been given human form, a divine animal becoming an anthropomorphic deity. Lucan speaks of a god Taranis placated by human sacrifices, and a scholiast on the passage identifies him with Dispater. Images of a benevolent-looking deity with a hammer and cup, sometimes called Sucellos, have also been regarded as representing Dis. The type of the images is similar to that of underworld deities elsewhere.

Esus, mentioned by Lucan as worshipped with cruel rites, was identified by his scholiasts with the Celtic Mars or Mercury. He is known otherwise only from an altar found at Paris and on it he is depicted cutting down a tree. Here again conjecture has been busy with theories regarding him. Lucan's third deity, placated with similar cruelties, was Teutatis, from *teuta*, "tribe." He was thus a tribal deity, regarded by the scholiasts as Mars or Mercury. Similar names on inscriptions in Gaul and Britain equate him with Mars.

While there are dedications to Hercules alone or with other deities, e.g., Epona, there are few in which he is equated with a native deity. But according to Lucian the Celts called Hercules Ogmios, represented as an old man with a lion's skin, who holds enchained to his tongue by their ears a crowd of people. A Celt had explained this by saying that Ogmios had conquered men, not by strength of arm, but by the power of reason, and was represented as old because age alone is reasonable. There may be a possible connexion with the Irish god Ogma (p. 44). The head of Ogmios is figured on coins of the Ossismi.

The Roman wood god Silvanus is named on many inscriptions, especially in the Danube region, but he is also a deity of the house and Silvanus domesticus is named on several inscriptions. What native god or gods he represents is unknown, but Esus has been suggested. In addition there were grouped deities or spirits, Silvani and Silvanae.

Goddesses were worshipped, either as consorts of gods or as individuals, like the native Minervas. But as the earlier worship of the spirits of places gradually gave way to the worship of these as deities, we find the latter grouped together, and usually with Roman names rather than with native Celtic names. Thus there are grouped goddesses called Proxumae, "near to men," protectresses, Junones, sometimes with the epithet *domesticae*, also protectresses; Suleviae; Quadriviae, associated with cross-roads; Dominae, connected with the home; but especially the Matres or Mothers, usually three in number, but sometimes two or one. They are known from numerous inscriptions and monuments. Their cult was popular and widespread, in Gaul, in Britain, and in parts of Germany. They may be regarded as a threefold aspect of an earlier earth or fertility goddess, and an inscription from Britain calls them *Matres campestrae*. But their functions became wider. They guarded individuals, families (cf. the epithet *domesticae*), towns, provinces, even a whole nation. Akin to them are the Matronae, perhaps a Celtic rather than a Latin word, who may originally have been river-spirits, like another group, the Niskae, their name being connected with such river names as Marne. The inscriptions on which the Matronae occur are mainly from Cisalpine Gaul. The Matres survive in the three-fold fays of much later times. An interesting parallel is found in one Welsh name for the fairies, Y Mamau, "the mothers," as shown by Prof. Anwyl. The name "Mothers" existed in Ireland and some of the goddesses there had triple forms. The monuments of the Matres show them holding a child, baskets of fruit, a cornucopia, emblems of fertility.

It is possible that in the earlier life of the Celts, goddesses held a more important place than gods, possibly because the arts of civilization were mostly in the hands of women, who would naturally have female deities to watch over their activities. Even goddesses of war were known in Gaul, Britain, and Ireland, though in Gaulish inscriptions they are usually associated with Celtic forms of Mars. But Andrasta was a war goddess of the British people ruled by Boudicca (Boadicea). To her this queen prayed and human victims were sacrificed. The Irish war-goddesses will be considered later.

Some goddesses seem to have been connected with fertility, perhaps originally Earth-goddesses. Others again are river goddesses—Sequana, of the Seine; Abnoba, whose name is found in that of rivers called Avon; Divona, of rivers called Dee and the like, and others.

A goddess Epona, whose name is derived from *epos*, "horse," was known over a wide area. There are many representations of her, usually riding a horse or seated among horses. Here we have a goddess of horses, mules, asses, and these were reared by the Gauls, but Epona may first have been a horse as a worshipful animal. If she presided over the fertility of these creatures, this would connect her with fertility-goddesses generally, and she is sometimes represented with the symbols associated with the Matres. She may possibly at first have been a rushing river symbolized by a horse.

An interesting glimpse of the cult of a goddess of fertility is found at the time when Gaul was becoming Christian, towards the end of the fourth century. The image of this goddess was carried in procession on a chariot through fields and vineyards, the people singing before it. This cult continued till the time of Gregory of Tours.

CHAPTER V

THE DEITIES OF THE BRITISH CELTIC TRIBES

As Britain was in close contact with Gaul we might expect that some of their deities were alike. Inscriptions help us here, though it is well to bear in mind that some of these may be due to Gaulish soldiers enlisted in the Roman army and quartered in Britain. There are some examples of deities equated with Apollo, e.g., Anextiomarus, Grannos, Mogons or Mogounos (a sky- or sun-god), and Maponus.

Others, equated with Mars, are Camulos, who appears on coins with warlike emblems, and Belatucadros. Totatis is a probable equivalent of Teutatis, a tribal god, perhaps of war. Nodons, who had a temple on the Severn, where some of the symbols suggest his being a Celtic Neptune, has a name which means "riches" or "wealth," which he may have been supposed to impart to his worshippers. His name resembles that of the Irish Nuada and the Welsh Nudd (p. 43). Belenos, a sun-god (*belos*, "bright") appears as a warlike King in Geoffrey of Monmouth's *History*—the god regarded in later view as a king. Geoffrey says that the Billingsgate in London was so called because his ashes were preserved there—a reference to a widespread custom of burying a hero at a town gate in order to preserve it. Belenos may have survived as the Beli of the Welsh *Mabinogion*.

Andrasta, goddess of victory of the Iceni, is not known in inscriptions from Gaul, unless she is the Andarta of the Vocontii there. Sul and Belisama have already been referred to. Dea Brigantia, equated like these with Minerva, occurs on several inscriptions as the tribal goddess of the important Celtic people in North-East England, the Brigantes, and she may be an equivalent of the Irish Brigit (p. 42). Epona is frequently met with, as are also the Matres.

Much more information, at least concerning the divinities of the Brythons in Wales, is found in the Welsh *Mabinogion*. It

consists of stories which, if put together at a comparatively late
date, contain material of an earlier period. Its personages are
kings, queens, heroic beings, but there is general agreement
that some of them represent earlier deities. Other Welsh
documents contain similar relics of the past. The problem of
the origin of some of the personages of these tales, whether
arising from an earlier Goidelic occupation in Wales or Goidelic
influence on the people there, or as purely Brythonic, has been
much discussed. Though some of the persons of the tales
have Irish equivalents, most of them appear to be Brythonic.
Where a Goidelic equivalence exists it will be noted. The
Mabinogion consists of four prose narratives or "branches."
Possibly because of some consciousness of the real personality
of most of the characters, these narratives are full of mythical
incidents, magic, and the supernatural.

The *Mabinogi* of Pwyll, prince of Dyved, tells how he and
Arawn, prince of Annwfn, agreed to exchange their appearances
and their kingdoms for a year. When the year elapsed Pwyll
was ever after known as Pwyll Pen Annwfn, i.e., Head of
Annwfn. A later incident tells how he met on a magic mound
Rhiannon, who became his wife. Following her advice Pwyll
overcame Gwal fab Clud, who had demanded her in marriage,
enclosing him in a magic bag. Rhiannon's child was afterwards
spirited away, but found by Teyrnon, lord of Gwent. As the
child grew apace his likeness to Pwyll was noted. Teyrnon
took him to Pwyll, and Rhiannon, who had been disgraced, was
reinstated. The child was called Pryderi and eventually
succeeded his father as lord of Dyved.

Pwyll, as Pen Annwfn, is lord of the underworld, for
Annwfn means this, though here it is treated as a district on
the earth's surface. Pryderi also became its lord. They seem
thus to be deities of the Brythonic underworld, but, like other
underworld deities, associated with fertility. Rhiannon is an
earlier goddess, her name being resolved into Rigantona,
"great queen." Teyrnon's name is equivalent to Tigernonos
or "King," hence it has been suggested that Teyrnon and
Rhiannon, in one version or in an old myth, were parents of
Pryderi.

In the *Mabinogi* of Branwen, she is sister of Bran the

Blessed, for whom no. house had ever been large enough, and of Manawyddan, both sons of Llyr. They have two half-brothers, Nissyen and Evnissyen. Branwen was besought in marriage by Matholwych, King of Ireland. This was agreed to, but Evnissyen, whose consent had not been asked, mutilated Matholwych's horses. To make amends for this Bran gave the outraged king horses, gold, and a magic cauldron which would resuscitate all the dead thrown into it. Matholwych and Branwen went off, but in a year she was reduced to a menial position because of Evnissyen's outrage. Bran waded to Ireland, his men crossing in ships. In the sequel he was wounded by a poisoned spear, and, giving his followers instructions to cut off his head, died. The head was to be buried at the White Hill at London, looking towards France. Two of its bearers were Manawyddan and Pryderi. They spent seven years in a feast at Harlech, where the birds of Rhiannon entertained them, then eighty years at Gwales, where the head caused these to seem but as a day. Finally it was buried at London as Bran had directed.

Llyr, father of Bran and Manawyddan, is a form of the Irish Ler, god of the sea. He was father also of Creiddylad or Cordelia, and was later regarded as King of Britain, and is Shakespeare's King Lear. Manawyddan is a form of the splendid Irish sea-god Manannan, son of Ler. A Welsh poem makes him lord of Elysium, as Manannan was. He is described as a craftsman. Branwen, "White Bosom," may be the form of an earlier goddess, perhaps of love and fertility. As Brangwine in the Romances she gave a love potion to Tristram. Bendegeit Vran or "Bran the Blessed," to give him his full title, was later included among Welsh saints, but he also may have been an earlier divinity. The story of his head is significant. This Urdawl Ben or "Noble Head," causes the supernatural lapse of time to its bearers. The purpose of its burial is to prevent the land being invaded. As he is connected with music, carrying his musicians on his back to Ireland, he may have been a god worshipped by bards, and also connected with the Celtic other-world, where, as in the company of his head, a long period passes in what seems a short time. The burial of his head as a means of defence to the land is connected with customs concerning relics of the dead which still possessed power or with sculptured divine heads or images. The magic cauldron which restores the dead to life, is one of many such cauldrons associated with fertility in Celtic story.

The *Mabinogi* of Manawyddan carries on the story of Branwen. She had died of a broken heart. Caswallawn, son of Beli, had seized the Kingdom. Manawyddan and Pryderi were two of the seven bearers of Bran's head, and Pryderi now gave his mother Rhiannon to Manawyddan as wife, possibly a memory of the fact that these were a divine pair, with Pryderi as their son. Pryderi had been married to Kicva, and they with Manawyddan and Rhiannon continued together. Then Pryderi and Rhiannon disappeared along with a magic castle into which they had entered. This disappearance was caused by the magician Llwyt, in revenge for the insult done by Pwyll to Gwal. Manawyddan overcame this magician, and Pryderi and Rhiannon were restored. Throughout this tale we find Manawyddan overcoming wizards and instructing Pryderi in various crafts, besides practising agriculture. These may connect him with the Celtic Elysium, and, as has been seen, he is called its lord in a Taliesin poem. This position was true of the Irish Manannan also. Casswallawn, whose name is found in the historic Cassivellaunus, is described in one of the Welsh triads as "war king," and this suggests his having been a Brythonic war-god.

In the fourth branch, that of Math, we are told of Goewin, Math's virgin "foot-holder," and of two sons of Don, Gilvae-thwy and Gwydion. The former is in love with her. To aid him Gwydion went to Pryderi's court to obtain for Math certain swine which had been a gift of Arawn, King of Annwfn. He obtained these by a trick, and Pryderi and his forces invaded the land of Math, as Gwydion had intended. For now that Math is engaged in war, Gilvaethwy seduced Goewin. Math discovers this when the war, in which Pryderi is slain by Gwydion, whose expert magic brings this about, is ended. Math makes Goewin his wife. He avenges himself on Gilvaethwy and Gwydion by changing them for a year into deer, for a second year into swine, for a third year into wolves. When this punishment is over Gwydion proposed his sister Arianrhod as Math's foot-holder. She is not a virgin, however, and now has two sons. One of these was later killed by Govannon, another brother of Arianrhod. The other is nurtured by Gwydion, and he was brought to Arianrhod who said that he would never have a name. Through Gwydion's magic she does name him, Llew Llaw Gyffes. For him a wife, Blodeuwedd, was formed out of flowers. He is attacked by Gronw, her lover, wounded, and flies away in the form of an eagle. Gwydion found him, and he was restored to his lands, and turned Blodeuwedd into an owl.

Of the characters in this long tale, in which magic plays a large part, Math Hen, or the aged, himself a supreme magician, is to be regarded as an important god of Gwyned, of which he is lord. He is shown to be kindly and just, therefore a beneficent deity.

But in Don, who plays no part in the tale, and her family Gwydion, Gilvaethwy, Govannon and Arianrhod, including also Arianrhod's sons, Dylan and Llew Llaw Gyffes, we have the relics of a divine group. They have a parallel, to some extent, in names and in functions, with the divine group in Ireland, the family of the goddess Danu. Llew has some parallel with the Irish Lug, Govannon with Goibniu, Gwydion is master of magic as well as a mighty bard, and brings swine from the divine land. We may see in him a culture-god, a kind of Mercury. The name of Govannon, like that of the Irish Goibniu, means "smith," and like Goibniu he may be regarded as a divine artificer, a god of metal-workers. Arianrhod, if an earlier goddess, may have been an earth-goddess, and, like most of these, at once a virgin and a fruitful mother. About Llew Llaw Gyffes there has been much theorizing to the effect that he, like the Irish Lug, was a sun-god, and that their names and epithets are equivalent. This is by no means certain. Dylan or Dylan Eil Ton, "Son of the Wave," who rushes into the sea, and of whom it is said that the waves mourn for him, was identified popularly with the waves, and he may be regarded as a god of the sea. A triad speaks of Beli as father of Arianrhod. Was he Don's consort? This is not certain, but he may be a form of the god Belenos.

It is significant of the importance attached to the personages of the *Mabinogion* that three of them are connected with the stars. The Milky Way was called Caer Gwydion, the constellation Cassiopeia was called the Court of Don, and Arianrhod was connected with the constellation Corona Borealis.

The poems attributed to the poet Taliesin and the story called *Hanes Taliesin* contain some evidence about the deities. In the poems Taliesin connects himself with these, and much of what he says belongs to what was remembered of a deity who bore his name, and whom he figures himself to be, a god of poetic inspiration. The story, *Hanes Taliesin*, is based on a folk-tale formula, that of the Transformation Combat, in which the protagonists successively take different shapes, continuing their fight in each. Here we have a divine pair, Tegid Voel and Cerridwen. They, with their children, the beautiful Creirwy, Morvran, and the ugly Avagddu, dwell in Lake Tegid. Cerridwen, to benefit Avagddu with knowledge, prepared "a cauldron of inspiration." Three drops of its contents would give the required knowledge. Gwion was set to watch the cauldron; the three drops fell on his finger which he put to his mouth, thus acquiring the inspiration. He fled, pursued by Cerridwen. In different forms they fought. Finally Gwion, as a grain of wheat, was swallowed by her in the shape she had taken, that of a hen, and later he was born of her. She threw him into the sea, whence Elphin rescued him, and he became the greatest of bards. From other sources we gather that Taliesin could change his form and had frequently been reborn. He had a "splendid chair" in Caer Sidi or Elysium, which chair is "the inspiration of fluent song." In another poem, he with Arthur and others go overseas to Caer Sidi to obtain "the spoils of Annwfn," which included the cauldron of Pen Annwfn, lord of Elysium. Here we have traces of a myth, with many parallels elsewhere, telling how gifts of civilization are stolen by culture-heroes from the divine land for the benefit of mortals.

The waters in which Tegid and his family dwell reveal him and Cerridwen as deities of these, possibly of an underwater Wonderland. The cauldron is one of many spoken of in Celtic story, a familiar property of the divine land. It produces regeneration and knowledge and is inexhaustible. It may be regarded as having to do with fertility. Cerridwen may thus be a goddess of fertility or, again, of inspiration, a goddess dear to bards, just as Taliesin is the divine bard.

Morvran, whose name means "sea crow," may have been a local war-god. In Irish myth there were goddesses of war who appeared as scald-crows. Morvran was called "support of battle."

Much has been written of Arthur and the Arthurian poems and romances, so popular from the twelfth century onwards. Some at least of the personages of these may have been earlier Brythonic deities, and possibly there was a local Brythonic deity called by a name like Arthur. But there was a historic British hero Arthur, almost certainly a King or warrior of the Brythons of lowland Scotland, some of whom migrated to Wales, carrying his story with them. There he may have been fused with Arthur the deity, and soon became the hero of the Arthurian romances. What can be known of Arthur as a deity or, possibly, a culture-hero? His name has been held to be Artor, "ploughman," which would make him primarily a god of agriculture. An equivalent of the name has been seen in Artaios, a god of Gaul, equated with Mercury. But the link with the historic Arthur might rather make him a war-god.

The mythic Arthur is found in the Welsh tale of *Kulhwch and Olwen*. Kulhwch is set the task of capturing Twrch Trwyth, or Porcus Troit, a hero transformed to a boar, between whose ears were scissors, razor and comb. To do this the aid of Mabon had to be gained, and he had been in an unknown prison since his birth. Arthur released him, and now the pursuit of the boar began. Arthur fought it for nine days, but failed to kill it. A further hunt began and in time the three objects in its ears were gained. Next the blood of the sorceress Gorddu had to be obtained and she was slain by Arthur.

Some of the personages of the *Mabinogion*, as well as of the romantic Arthur cycle, are found in this tale. Of the latter are Kei, Bedwyr (Bedivere), Gwalchmei (Gawain), and Gwenhwyfar (Guinevere). Mabon, from *mab*, *map*, "a youth," is a memory of the Gaulish and British god Maponos, equated with Apollo. His mother is called Modron, a name which suggests Matrona. Apart from references to Kei in the romances, he is spoken of in Welsh poetry as a great warrior, greater even than Arthur, as Gwenhwyfar said. Even in *Kulhwch* his powers are of a superhuman kind, and no wound caused by him could be healed. If he was originally a deity, he may have been a local war-god. Gwenhwyfar, if her name means "white phantom" or "fairy," resembles Irish female beings, of a white or fairy aspect, who were goddesses. She may thus have been an earlier deity.

Merlin or Myrddin, who figures prominently in the Romances, bard, prophet, magician, but especially magician, has been regarded on slender grounds as a Celtic Zeus. Much more likely he was the Brythonic ideal magician or even god of magicians. Most of what is said of him in the Romances throws little light on his personality.

CHAPTER VI

THE DEITIES OF THE GOIDELS IN IRELAND

THERE is a large body of Irish documents, mainly of the medieval period, Annals, heroic tales of many kinds, poems, from which our knowledge of the Irish deities is obtained. The annalists, writing in Christian times, had earlier documents and also traditional lore on which to draw. They told of the supposed invasions of Ireland by various groups, ending with the Milesians. Their aim was to prove the ancestry of these groups, and to connect them with Biblical personages, e.g., Noah. It is certain also that they transformed the deities into kings, queens, heroes. Among the groups named by them are Firbolgs, Fir-Domnann, and Galioin, Fomorians, Tuatha Dé Danann, and Milesians.

Of these groups the first three are best regarded as representing the aboriginal peoples of Ireland, previous to the coming of the Goidelic Celts, and the Fomorians as their deities. The Fomorians were said to have been defeated by the Tuatha Dé Danann. Though the Milesians are described as having conquered the Tuatha Dé Danann, these were the deities of the Milesians. All groups alike are treated by the annalists as mortals, though the supernatural traits of those who had not been mortals were not easily explained. These Christian annalists were not certain how to treat the group known as Tuatha Dé Danann. They had been banished from heaven, they were phantoms, they were demons, yet were described as mortals. The defeated Tuatha Dé Danann were supposed to have retreated into the *síd* or mounds, where they lived as a kind of fairy race with many of their older divine aspects. This was certainly a popular tradition.

The annalists, with their view that all earlier groups, actual, imaginary, or divine, were human, and possibly knowing that some of them had actually been deities, changed the actual fact of the introduction of Christianity as the cause of the collapse of the deities of the pagan past, into their defeat, as mortals, by actual mortals, the Milesians. As many tales and traditions show, the people regarded the deities now as a kind of fairy folk, who might even now be appealed to by them in time of need. Yet, in some documents, which set the annalistic scheme at defiance, the gods appear as still powerful deities long after the Milesians conquered them. But their day was drawing to a close. Christianity, represented by St. Patrick and others, will overcome their power. They will be sent to the hills and rocks, or perhaps one might be seen, a god in exile, wandering among men. This is stated in the interesting and non-annalistic *Colloquy of the Ancients*. This book contains much traditional matter, and it dates from the thirteenth century, showing that myths and traditions lived on long after the coming of Christianity.

Part of the annalistic scheme deals with the defeat of the Firbolgs, though with difficulty, by the Tuatha Dé Danann. The Firbolgs were slaves and have many contemptuous epithets attached to them. They are to be regarded, as has been said, as representing the pre-Celtic folk of Ireland. The Fomorians are actually called their deities. The annalistic account of the defeat and subjection of Firbolgs and others by the Tuatha Dé Danann must be based on traditions of the overcoming of the pre-Celtic peoples by Celtic invaders, aided by their deities.

The annalists regarded the Fomorians as pirates or sea-demons, deriving their name from *muir*, "sea," as do some modern scholars. Though regarded sometimes as essentially dark and demoniac they must originally have been more or less beneficent deities of the pre-Celtic people, but regarded in an opposite manner by the Celts.

The annalistic accounts of the relations between Fomorians and Tuatha Dé Danann are curious. Both are regarded as human and as kings, yet their supernatural aspect is not forgotten. Some of them unite in marriage, as members of hostile tribes sometimes do. Nuada, leader of the Tuatha Dé Danann, lost his hand, though it was later replaced by a silver hand, and as a king with a blemish was impossible, the crown was given to the Fomorian Bres. Two battles at Magtured between Fomorians and Tuatha Dé Danann are recorded, with a period of twenty-seven years elapsing between them, but in earlier annalistic schemes, possibly there was one battle only. But whether one or two these battles are to be regarded as signifying the final superiority of the gods of the Celts to those of the aborigines, and the Fomorians, undoubtedly deities of fertility, came to be regarded as dark, hostile beings. In the second battle Bres was captured, and he offered, to save his life, that cows should always give milk and that there should be a harvest every quarter. These offers were refused, but, on his promising to tell how the men of Erin should plough, sow and reap, he was set free. This surely suggests that he was an earlier god of fertility. Balor, a Fomorian, seems, however, to be a personification of the evil eye. His eye had become poisonous through the fumes of a magic potion. When four men raised his eyelid on a battlefield, none could resist his baleful gaze. Lug, one of the Tuatha Dé Danann, destroyed his eye with a stone.

Whatever the Fomorians may have been, an evil character is ascribed to them by the annalists. The Tuatha Dé Danann are regarded more sympathetically. They came from heaven, says one account, which fits in well with their divine character. They know magic; they possess magic treasures, e.g., the inexhaustible cauldron of Dagda, the matchless spear of Lug, the unconquerable sword of Nuada. While they are regarded as mortals, as kings, their divinity is often breaking in. A remarkable example of this appears in a story of St. Patrick. One of their number was seen with Fian Caoilte by the saint. He asked why she was beautiful and young, while Fian was decrepit. Her answer was that Fian was mortal and perishable, while she was of the Tuatha Dé Danann, unfading and of perennial duration.

While the Tuatha Dé Danann, "the people of the goddess Danu," or the Tuatha Dea, "people of the goddess," are regarded as a group under this goddess, she is not actually mother of all of them, but of three sons, Brian, Iuchar, and Iucharbar, who are called, perhaps by a mistaken etymology, gods of *dan* or "knowledge." In one place they are said to have been *dei terreni*, worshipped before St. Patrick's time. They are connected with the whole group by the title sometimes given to the Tuatha Dé Danann, *Fir tri ndea,* "men of the three gods." Some incidents suggest that they had a high place, e.g., Dagda, Ogma, and Lug, three of the gods, take their advice. But on the whole their functions are obscure.

Danu is made daughter of Dagda by the annalists, and one old writer, Cormac, describes Anu as "mother of the deities of the Irish." Perhaps Anu and Danu were one and the same, for while Cormac calls two hills in Kerry "the paps of Anu," a later gloss gives "the paps of Danu." Anu, it is said, was worshipped as a goddess of plenty. Possibly she or Danu was an earth-goddess. The fruits of the earth, their roots below the surface, were gifts of earth deities.

Another goddess, more popular than Danu, was Brig or Brigit, knowledge (*dan*), culture, and poetry being her province. Hence she was sometimes identified with Danu. According to later accounts there were three Brigits, the two others being associated with smith-work and leech-craft. Brigit, or a goddess with similar name and functions, was known in Gaul and Britain, in the former Brigindu, in the latter, Brigantia. As a goddess of culture and poetry she is a form of the Gaulish deities equated by Cæsar with Minerva. She may have belonged to a period when the Celts worshipped goddesses rather than gods, or, at least, gave them a high place. Aspects of her personality and cult are seen in the immensely popular Irish and West Highland saint of the same name (or sometimes Bride). According to Giraldus Cambrensis, the saint had a sacred fire at Kildare. No male might approach it. Nineteen nuns guarded it in turn, and on the twentieth day the saint herself, though dead. This, if not actual custom connected with the cult of St. Brigit, must be a tradition of a fire sacred to the goddess and guarded by priestesses. Brigit would then be an equivalent of Sul at Bath, in whose temple perpetual fires burned. Sul was equated with Minerva, and Brigit was evidently a goddess of the same kind.

War-goddesses had an important place among the Irish Celts. They appeared in the form of scald-crows, seen near the slain on battlefields. The name of this bird, *badb,* was given to one of the goddesses, who are three in number, but the name may be generic. She is identified with Morrigan, "great queen" or possibly "night-mare queen." Macha and Neman are the names of the others. Cæsar mentions a Gaulish commander, Boduognatus, "born of Bodua," and Cathubodua occurs on an inscription, the equivalent of the Irish Badbcatha, "battle-crow," another name of the goddess. This suggests that a goddess of similar name was known in Gaul. There were war-gods among the Irish, but these goddesses may be more primitive, and we have to remember that women went to battle in Ireland.

Of the gods Dagda occupied a high place. He was known as "lord of great knowledge" and as "great father" to the Tuatha Dé Danann. One text speaks of him as "the chief god of the pagans." His functions are obscure, but he may once have been an earth-god, a god of fertility, as some things told of him suggest, and possibly an Irish Dispater. He had a cauldron which never failed to satisfy; swine, of which one was always living and one ready for cooking; and trees always laden with fruit. He was lord of a *síd* or mound, a form of the Celtic Wonderland, and in it were these unfailing things. His consort was Boand; his children Brigit, Danu, Oengus, Bodb Dearg, and Ogma, but these filiations are not necessarily accurate.

When the Tuatha Dé Danann, according to the annalistic account, were defeated by the Milesians, Dagda divided the *síd* or mounds among the deities, and into these they retired. In one story Oengus expelled Dagda from his *síd* and ruled there. This unfilial conduct may reflect some tradition of a cult of Oengus becoming more popular than that of Dagda, or that he was god of a tribe who had conquered another tribe, worshippers of Dagda. Oengus Mac ind Oc, "son of the young ones," i.e., Dagda and Boand, who appears in several romantic tales, is one of the most attractive of the Irish deities. He was perhaps a god of fertility, but this is uncertain. In the Fionn heroic cycle he is the fosterer of Diarmaid. Nuada, who lost his hand in the first battle of Magtured, and on that account ceased to be king of the Tuatha Dé Danann until Diancecht made him a silver hand, was hence called Nuada Argetlam, "of the silver hand." He has been regarded as equivalent of

Lludd Llawereint, "the silver handed," in Welsh story, and may be connected with the British god Nodons.

Lug, whose appearance suggested that of the sun in one account of the fight with the Fomorians, appears in another as master of many crafts, superior to each and all of the divine craftsmen. Hence his epithet *samildanach*, "inventor of all arts." This recalls Cæsar's description of the Gaulish Mercury, and the cult of Lug may have existed among more than one branch of the Celtic people. Luguvallum, "wall of Lugus," is connected with Hadrian's wall, and in Gaul there was Lugudunum (Lyons), "stronghold of Lugus." These attest a widespread cult, and at Lugudunum there was a festival in August corresponding to an Irish festival at the same time called Lugnasad. Was Lug a sun-god or was he a supreme culture-god, superior to all lesser culture or craft deities? Among the latter are gods of metal-work, an important branch of culture among the Celts. One of these was Creidne, from *cerd*, "artificer," the divine brazier. Another was Diancecht, a god of medicine, famous for his healing powers, who, with Creidne's help, fashioned Nuada's silver hand. There was also Goibniu (*goba*, "smith") who made spears which could not fail to kill, and whose skill is a reflection of the skilled work of human smiths and metal-workers. Luchtine was god of carpenters and, at the battle of Magtured, made spear-shafts, fitting them accurately into the spear-heads.

Ogma was a god of poetry and eloquence, his name being extended as Mac Elathan, "son of knowledge." At the battle of Magtured he appears as champion of the Tuatha Dé Danann. Another epithet of his is *grianainech*, "of the smiling face," recalling Lucian's description of the Gaulish Ogmios, god of eloquence, who also has a smiling face (page 29). Here we see a widespread cult of one and the same god. Bardic eloquence and poetry were honoured among the Celts.

Little is known of Ler, "sea," a god of the sea, equivalent of the Welsh Llyr. Much more prominent is his son Manannan, also connected with the sea, and the equivalent of the Welsh Manawyddan. His cult seems to have been more prominent than that of Ler, and later tradition spoke of four Manannans, local forms of the same god. One of those was connected with the Isle of Man, where tradition placed his grave. One document asserts that both Britons and Irish held him to be god of the sea, which agrees with the Manannan-Manawyddan identification. Various tales show his connexion with the sea. He is a great sea-wave, or he rides on the waves or on a chariot which crosses them, and the waves were called "the son of Ler's horses." He was associated with the island Wonderland or with that as situated on earth. Manannan is said to have given the gods immortality and magic food. Among his possessions were swine which resumed life after being slain, armour which made the wearer invulnerable, a sword, terrifying all who saw it. He appears in the heroic sagas of Cúchulainn and Fionn. Folk-tradition still remembers him, and he was evidently a popular deity.

On the whole the Tuatha Dé Danann were deities of fertility, agriculture, the arts of civilization, and war. Those named here need not represent all the deities of the Irish Celts. There would be many local gods, with similar functions, and some of these may have been absorbed in those whose names have survived.

These also bear other names, perhaps those of similar deities assimilated to them. Local deities are suggested in such references as speak of the god of Connaught, the god of Ulster, and the like. Besides a general power over fertility, the functions of the deities had a wider scope, and to all of them magical possessions are ascribed in the documents which tell of them. Even when they are regarded as merely mortals, these magic possessions are still spoken of. They survive in a world of fancy, romance, and magic.

As has been seen from the annalistic account, the defeated Tuatha Dé Danann, or their surviving members, retreated to dwell in the mounds, some of which still exist, tumuli or ancient burial-places. The conquest of the gods, envisaged as mortals, is an attempt to put in quasi-historical form the victory of the Christian faith over paganism. But paganism was not expelled completely, for the Tuatha Dé Danann still survived as a kind of fairy-folk dwelling in the mounds. This, and the story of their retiring into the mounds after their defeat, can only mean that once they were worshipped at mounds or hills, or were somehow connected with these or with underground places all of which were wonderful places, their immortal abodes, like the remote islands with which they were also connected, as some stories show. The gods, made into mortals by the annalists, were also supposed to be buried in the mounds.

CHAPTER VII

MYTHICAL HEROES

CÚCHULAINN, "the hound of Culann," is the hero, almost a demigod, of a large number of tales, culminating in a long story, the Táin Bó Cuailgne, or "Cattle Raid of Cooley." He is the hero of Ulster, of which Conchobar was king, who died at the time of our Lord's Crucifixion. Conchobar, who is called *dia talmaide*, "terrestrial god," was related to Cúchulainn, because his sister Dechtire was the hero's mother. Conchobar was the son of Nessa, daughter of one of the Tuatha Dé Danann, and Cathbad, but in an earlier account of his birth he is said to have had the god Lug for a father. Lug is brought into connexion with Cúchulainn also. He is son of a more or less shadowy Sualtam, but there is a suggestion that he was the son of Dechtire through an incestuous union with Conchobar. But the god Lug is also said to be his father, while, again, Cúchulainn appears as a re-birth of the god himself. He was called Setanta, but later received his name Cúchulainn from an exploit in which he slew a watch-dog of Culann's, and then offered himself to act as watch-dog.

Cúchulainn's growth was rapid and even as a boy he was extraordinary for his strength, and became famous for his "distortion" or battle frenzy. When this came upon him, he was plunged into three successive vats of cold water in order to overcome it, but the water itself boiled from the heat which he gave out. From his earliest years he fought and overcame heroes and champions, but his strange "distortion" caused the death of many, for then his very look was fatal. There is a curious account of a strange weakness which befell the warriors of Ulster when their strength was most needed, called the weakness of the men of Ulster. It was the result of a curse put upon them by Macha, one of the war-goddesses, who, when pregnant, had been compelled to run a race with Conchobar's horses, one of the strange anomalous tales about deities. From this weakness Cúchulainn was exempt, for he was not really an Ulsterman, but the son of the god Lug.

In his early youth he went to Alba (Scotland) to visit Scathach, so that his warrior skill might be increased through her tuition. After many perils he reached her castle on a rock, separated from the mainland. He leaped the gulf and landed safely. Now began his tuition, and he not only conquered Aife, the rival of Scathach, but begat a son by her, bidding her call the child Connla when born. Long after, Cúchulainn, unaware of who an opponent was, slew him. He was Connla. This is a version of an episode which appears in other mythologies, the slaying of a son by his father. When Cúchulainn returned to Ireland, he attacked Forgall who, because of his love for Emer his daughter, had caused him to go to Scathach, believing that he would not survive the dangers. Now Forgall was slain, and Emer became Cúchulainn's wife.

One of the many adventures ascribed to the hero is his visit to the divine land. The goddess Fand, deserted by its ruler Manannan, promised him her love if he would help her brother-in-law Labraid against his foes. Cúchulainn sent his charioteer to reconnoitre, and he returned with news of the land's wonderful trees with fruit which nourished hundreds, its vat of ale which never grew less, its attractiveness, above all the beauty of Fand. This determined the hero to go thither. He overcame Labraid's enemies and remained for a month with Fand. The rest of the tale relates to a contest between Fand, who had come to meet the hero, and his wife Emer. In the sequel Manannan, "the horseman of the crested sea-waves," appeared. He shook his mantle between Fand and Cúchulainn, so that they could not meet again.

It is impossible to cite the many tales in which Cúchulainn appears. Some are long and rambling like *Fled Bricrend* or "Bricrui's Feast." We turn to the most important part of the Cúchulainn cycle, the *Táin Bó Cuailgne,* which is itself prefaced by preparatory tales. The deities Ochall and Bodb had each a swine herd, Friuch and Rucht. They quarrelled, and continued their fight in various forms into which they had transformed themselves. In their final transformation they became worms each of which was swallowed by a cow. They were now reborn as bulls, Find Bennach, "Whitehorn," and the Brown Bull of Cuailgne called Donn. Whitehorn came into possession of Medb, queen of Connaught, who had once been wife of Conchobar. She desired to obtain the Brown Bull, but she failed in this and an immense army was raised to invade Ulster, just when its warriors were suffering from their weakness. Cúchulainn engaged in single combat with several of Medb's heroes. His wounds were many, but Lug helped him, and herbs of healing were thrown into the streams in which he washed his wounds by some of the Tuatha Dé Danann. Then the Ulstermen recovered from their weakness and defeated Medb's forces. But the Brown Bull had been captured by her and sent to Connaught, where it fought Whitehorn, killed it, and rushed to Ulster with its mangled body impaled on its horns. There it perished, charging a rock which, in its fury, it believed to be another bull.

Cúchulainn's death was the result of his breaking one of his tabus or *geasa*, never to eat dog's flesh. As he went to his final battle with his enemies he was persuaded to do this. His strength left him and he perished in the fight.

Attempts have been made to prove that Cúchulainn is a sun hero, but these are not conclusive. Neither is the theory that certain monuments in Gaul have reference to Cúchulainn in the form of the god Esus, and to the bull there shown as the Bull of Cuailgne. Rather is he to be regarded as the idealized hero of warrior people, viewed mythically and endowed with superhuman powers, and into whose history, as told in so many tales, have been drawn some of the deities as well as many strange and mythical fancies.

Another hero, Fionn, with a group of warriors surrounding him, is found in the numerous stories which comprise the Fionn Saga, located mainly in Munster and Leinster. The incoming of the Scots from Ireland into the highlands and islands of western Scotland, localized Fionn there also. The tales of Fionn and his group, the Feinne or Fians, belong to the third century A.D. By some it has been held that they were an actual warrior body maintained for the defence of Ireland. While it is not impossible that such an army existed, whatever links there may have been between it and Fionn and his heroes are worn thin by the action of the mythical personalities and the mythical doings ascribed to these. We regard them, therefore, as a group of mythical heroes who impressed themselves upon the minds and memories of Gaelic-speaking peoples. Not only so, but in many of the tales they are brought into contact with members of the Tuatha Dé Danann, the gods of the Irish Celts. Most of the tales belong to or are based upon doings of the pagan period, and throw some light upon the beliefs of that time.

Fionn was the son of Cumal, himself a mythical hero, who has been identified with Camulos, mentioned in inscriptions from Gaul, in which he is equated with Mars, and was therefore a war-god. The main personages of the cycle, apart from these, are Oisin (Ossian), son of Fionn; Oscar, his grandson, Diarmaid, his nephew, Fergus, Caoilte, Conan, a kind of Thersites, and other lesser personages. There is much that'is mythic and supernatural in the saga, much fighting, many strange adventures, hunting and love affairs.

After his father's death, Fionn became leader of the Feinne. It was told of him that in his youth he was set to cook "the salmon of knowledge" by the bard Finéces, but warned not to eat it. There were myths in Ireland about salmon in wells, which fed on wonderful nuts falling from trees above the well, and so became possessors of knowledge. These trees and wells were either on earth or in the divine land. Fionn became possessor of this knowledge, though for him it was not intended, just as inspiration was not meant for Gwion in the Welsh tale already cited. Fionn burnt his thumb while tending the salmon, put it in his mouth, and so fell heir to this knowledge. In future he had only to put his thumb in his mouth and the knowledge desired at the time was his. The boyish deeds of Fionn are the subject of many tales, and he soon became a a great warrior as well as a great lover.

A curious story was told of Oisin, about his mother's being changed to a deer and his being found by Fionn as a beast-child and cared for by him till he became human. Fionn himself had been a poet, but in this art Oisin excelled him. Fionn fought with giants and all kinds of monstrous beings, even with deities, though these sometimes helped him, as well as with Lochlanners, whether these were imaginary beings of a marine kind or Norsemen, the latter an anachronism, for the Norsemen did not come to Ireland until long after Fionn's time. If Norsemen, this meaning was given to them at a later time.

Fionn was betrothed to Grainne, the beautiful woman who, on seeing the handsome Diarmaid, whose *ball-seirc* or "beauty spot" made all women fall in love with him, fell a victim to his charm. Diarmaid was beloved by some of the gods, by Manannan, "with most potent Manannan thou studiedst and wast brought up in the Land of Promise," by Oengus, the Dagda's son, "thou wast most accurately taught," and Oengus afterwards gave him much needed help in his troubles. There are different versions of the story of Grainne's love, but what caused Diarmaid to flee with her was that she put *geasa* upon him to do this. *Geasa* had the meaning both of tabus and obligations. Diarmaid was thus obliged to elope with her. In his rage Fionn pursued them from place to place, but when he did capture them, the Feinne would not allow him to slay the hero. But Fionn bided his time and eventually caused Diarmaid's death by making him measure with his foot the length of the boar of Gulban. Now it was one of Diarmaid's *geasa* never to hunt a boar. One of the bristles pierced his foot and wounded him fatally, Fionn meanwhile withholding from him the water which he sorely needed.

Fionn himself and many of his band fell in fight. At last few but Oisin and Caoilte survived. There are several forms of a tale in which Oisin went to Tir na nOg or to a *síd*, remaining there for centuries, which seemed but a brief time. Then he returned to earth, and touching the soil, became old and feeble. Soon after he met St. Patrick. Caoilte also met the saint and told him many tales of Fionn. He was baptized, and St. Patrick interceded for Fionn and his relatives who were in hell. This tolerant attitude is found in the thirteenth century work, *Colloquy of the Ancients*, but quite a different attitude, saint and pagan hero hostile to each other, is found in other tales.

The vast collection of stories, ballads, poems about the Feinne, introducing us to a wild world of fighting, adventure, love, the supernatural, shows how deeply Fionn and his circle had impressed themselves on the Celts in Ireland, who carried the saga to the Western Isles of Scotland.

MacPherson's Ossianic epic worked like a charm on the European mind on and after its publication in 1762, though its author was fiercely attacked for pretending that it was translated from genuine Gaelic manuscripts. The controversy still has echoes in our day. What is certain is that the work as given to the world by him was not translated from a Gaelic original, but yet has points of greatness and originality which still commend it to readers.

CHAPTER VIII

WORSHIP AND ITS ACCESSORIES

T HE Celts were a religious people, "much given to religious practices," says Cæsar. He gives an example of the power of religious scruples in preventing action of a particular kind, when he says that Dummorix, a Gaulish chief, was prevented on religious grounds from going to Britain with him. The will of the gods was recognized, e.g., by the Cadurci in their defeat, which was not due to human cause, and such a belief in destiny is frequently observed in Irish documents.

Not much is known regarding the worship offered to the gods by the pagan Celts, but sacrifice had a large place in it. First, as to the sacrifice of animals. Arrian speaks of these among the Celts of Galatia. Money was put away, so much for each animal caught in hunting. With this was bought a calf, sheep, or goat, and the victims were sacrificed at a yearly festival of a goddess equated with Artemis. In Gaul there were also animal sacrifices. Cæsar speaks of living creatures taken as spoil in victory, along with other kinds of booty. All these were offered or dedicated to the Gaulish war-gods. In some districts heaps of booty were collected in sacred places. When anyone was found to have held back such spoil or to have dared to remove any from the pile, he was punished severely with torture. Such sacrifices may have been made to the deity or spirit of a river. When the Gauls conquered Mallius, the horses of the defeated were thrown into the Rhine. Such destruction of valuable booty was plainly sacrificial, an act of thanksgiving. In Ireland there is scanty evidence for animal sacrifice, but there is no doubt that it was practised, and there are examples of such sacrifices, e.g., to saints in later times, survivals of sacrifice to a deity. Animals must also have been sacrificed in time of cattle plague, for of this also there have been recorded local survivals.

Where sacrifice of animals was made, there was a feast on the sacrifice, a natural manner of coming into relation with the deity to whom the offering was made. Dio Chrysostom speaks of the Britons sacrificing and feasting. After the sacrifice to the local Artemis among the Galatian Celts, the worshippers and their dogs feasted, the dogs being decked with flowers.

There is sufficient evidence to show that human sacrifice, even on a large scale, was practised, and that this was often of a propitiatory kind. Illness or disease came upon men, calamities overtook them, there was defeat in war. Obviously the deities were offended with their worshippers; they must therefore be appeased, and it seemed that this was best done by the sacrifice of human victims. Cruel as this was, it was natural where human life was held of little value, and when the gods were regarded as implacable, and any means must be resorted to that their good humour might be restored. This will be seen from what Cæsar, Diodorus, and Strabo say, possibly all borrowing from an acute observer, Poseidonius.

Cicero reproached the Gauls for their human sacrifices, and Suetonius speaks of the detestable cruelty of Druidic religion. The Roman conquerors of Gaul were shocked at this aspect of the religion and severely repressed it, so that by the middle of the first century it had ceased.

The human victims were in the first place propitiatory, to appease angry gods, but they were also offered for thanksgiving. Even wives and children were sacrificed before a battle to ensure victory. Prisoners were immolated after a victory in thanksgiving to the gods—Lucan speaks of the cruel sacrifices offered by tribes in Gaul dwelling between the Seine and the Loire to such deities as Teutatis, Esus, and Taranis. Cæsar says that persons in extreme sickness or who are exposed to the perils of war, sacrifice human victims or vow to do so, employing the Druids to carry out the rite. They believe that unless a life is given for a life the majesty of the immortal gods cannot be appeased. Such sacrifices were made by private individuals or in public ceremonies. He speaks of one public ceremony which for horror cannot be surpassed. Figures of immense size, their limbs made of wicker, were filled with human victims, and set on fire. The victims pleasing to the gods were thieves or other criminals. Failing these, innocent victims were offered. As fire was the medium in which these victims perished,

it is possible that they were offered to a sun-god, with a view
of obtaining his fertilizing power.

Compare with this what Strabo says about human sacrifice.
Victims were shot with arrows or impaled in the temples. Or
a colossus of wood and straw was made and into it were thrown
animals and human beings. Of this and its contents were made
a fiery offering. Diodorus tells how criminals were kept for
five years, and then impaled as an offering to the gods. They
were dedicated along with offerings of first-fruits. Figures of
great size were made to contain the victims. Animals taken
as spoil in war and prisoners were burned or otherwise offered.
That such offerings consumed by fire were intended to promote
fertility is suggested by further words of Strabo's. Murderers
were turned over to the Druids. When there was a large supply
of these, evidently used as sacrificial victims, the Gauls
thought that there would be a large yield from the land.

All sacrifices were made with a Druid in attendance.

Thanksgivings should be offered to the gods by men
experienced in the nature of the divine, says Diodorus, and
who speak the language of the gods. Through such men they
think that blessings should be sought. Here we have a glimpse
of sacrifices of thanksgiving but Druids had to do with other
sacrifices also. Both Strabo and Diodorus speak of a human
victim being used for divining, the diviners having learned to
note results from ancient and long-continued practice in such
observations. The entrails of victims were consulted according
to some fixed and time-honoured method of observation. In
times of great gravity, says Diodorus, a human victim was
used. A dagger was plunged into him and the future was read
from the manner of his fall, the twitching of his limbs, and the
flow of blood. This is confirmed by Strabo. When the victim
used was human, libations were poured over him before the
actual slaying. Divination, especially by use of human victims,
was widespread over the Celtic area, and it was noted by
classical observers as one to which the Celts were more given
than any other nation.

There was also divination from observing the flight and the
cries of birds. When the Gauls were about to start on a hostile
expedition, their course was decided from the former, and

sometimes if the augury were inauspicious the expedition was abandoned for the time being. Dio Cassius tells how the forces of the Iceni were about to rise against the Romans, when their queen Boudicca, after haranguing them, let loose a hare which she had concealed in her garment. It fled in what was considered an auspicious direction, and the queen gave thanks to the tribal goddess Andrasta. The hare was a sacred animal among the Celts. Crows, in particular, were held to be birds of augury.

There was apparently a special class of men who practised divination, but it was certainly also used by the Druids, as examples recorded show, and Diodorus speaks of them in this capacity. In his work on divination Cicero speaks highly of a Druid of the Aedui, Diviciacus, known to him, who observed the course of nature and drew auguries, using also his own conjectures, about future events. Different kinds of prodigies in nature were regarded as omens.

Among the British Celts there is occasional evidence for human sacrifice, e.g., those victims offered to the goddess Andrasta. Tacitus speaks of the sacred groves in Anglesey being destroyed by the Romans to prevent a recurrence of the horrible rites practised there. The British tribes thought that their deities were pleased with these. The altars smoked with the blood of men, and the divine will was sought from their entrails.

Human sacrifice was prohibited throughout the Roman Empire by 97 B.C., but it was still practised in Britain in Pliny's time, A.D. 77.

As to the Irish Celts, human sacrifice is attested in some of the ancient documents. In St. Patrick's time, the first-born were offered at the Fair of Taillte and he preached against it. There was a deity called Cenn Cruaich, "head of the mound," and Cromm Cruaich, "the crooked one of the mound," possibly Dagda. One verse speaks of the people killing their children in order to pour blood round his image. The purpose of this was to obtain an abundance of milk and corn. The sacrifice took place at the winter festival. Another reference speaks of the violent aspect of the cult, "they beat their palms, they wounded their bodies, they shed showers of tears," and the prostrations of the worshippers were of a violent kind. The images of this god and his satellites had human form, and according to one legend, St. Patrick overthrew them.

There are occasional legendary notices of foundation sacrifices, i.e., the slaying of a human victim and burying the body under the foundation stones with a view to the stability of the building by propitiating the earth or earth deity and also to provide a spirit guardian for it. These legends are found in Britain and Ireland, and point to actual usage.

Some classical writers speak of the Celtic custom of cutting off the heads of prisoners and fixing them to the saddle-bows or on spears in a triumphal procession from the field of victory. The heads were offered to deities or to ancestors. Diodorus tells of their being fastened by nails to the doors of houses. Poseidonius had seen this; at first it sickened him, until he became accustomed to the sight. Skulls were found beneath an altar of one of the Celtic deities equated with Mars. Heads of outstanding enemies were embalmed or preserved in cedar oil and kept in a chest. Such heads were not given back even for ransom of an equivalent weight of gold. Heads were also placed on stakes. The Romans forbade this custom. Similar usages with heads existed among the Irish Celts, who called the heads of the slain "the mast of Macha," one of the war-goddesses.

The custom of drinking out of a skull may have been intended to gain the benefit of its former owner's qualities. The Boii cut off the head of the leader of their conquered foes, covered it with gold, and used it as a sacred vase for libations and as a drinking vessel for their chief priests.

There may have been a cult of the heads of noted men or ancestors. Such a custom may lie behind the story of Bran's head in the *Mabinogion*. After great delay, in which the head offered entertainment to its bearers, it was buried, as Bran had ordered, to guard the land from invasion.

Prayer to the gods was made with hands uplifted and was an adjunct of sacrifice and other ceremonies. It would be made in set formulas, as these were regarded as pleasing to the deities. Warriors advancing to battle sang war-chants composed by bards, and these, as well as the war-cries, would consist of invocation of a war deity.

TIMES OF RELIGIOUS IMPORTANCE

Divisions of the Celtic year were at first connected with agriculture and also with the seasons. But there is evidence that the Celts measured time by the moon, by lunar months. Thus Pliny says that the moon gave them the beginnings of months and years. Cæsar speaks of periods of time being determined by nights, not days, and that, with the Celts, night preceded day. Passages in Irish and Welsh texts confirm this. But the Druids, in so far as they studied astronomy, may have occupied themselves in adjusting the lunar to the solar years. Unfortunately, scarcely anything is known of seasonal festivals among the continental Celts: our information is mainly derived from Irish sources.

There was first a two-fold division of the year, a winter half and a summer half, beginning respectively with Samhain (our November 1st) and with Beltane (our May 1st). These two halves were then sub-divided, the second winter half beginning on February 1st, the second summer half on August 1st (Lugnasadh). There is evidence of ceremonial observances at Midsummer, but how that time was related to Beltane, the beginning of summer, is not clear. After the Christianizing of the Irish Celts some of the customs of these pagan festivals continued, but were now transferred to Christian feasts, e.g., Samhain was merged in All Saints' Day or transferred to St. Martin's Day, and the second winter quarter beginning with February 1st, with St. Brigit's or Bride's Day; Midsummer, with some of the Beltane ceremonial, with St. John Baptist's Day; Lugnasadh with Lammas.

There is little doubt that these festivals were intended primarily to assist the processes of growth and fertility, as the surviving customs show.

Samhain, which means "summer end," naturally pointed to the fact that the powers of blight, typified by winter, were beginning their reign. But it may have been partly a harvest festival, while it had connexion with pastoral activities, for the killing and preserving of animals for food during the winter was associated with it. The religious aspect of this may be difficult to see, but the later offering of one of the animals to

St. Martin in Ireland points to the sacrifice of one to a god in pagan times.

A bonfire was lit and represented the sun, the power of which was now waning, and the fire would be intended to strengthen it magically. People jumped through it, this act being intended to help them in sharing the sun's strength. In dwellings the fires were extinguished, a practice perhaps connected with the seasonal expulsion of evils. Branches were lit at the bonfire and carried into the houses to kindle the new fires. There is some evidence that a sacrifice, possibly human, occurred at Samhain, laden as the victim would be with the ills of the community, like the Hebrew scapegoat. The Irish texts speak of victims offered to the Fomorians and to the god known as Cromm Cruaich at Samhain. These sacrifices would appease hostile powers such as winter and blight were supposed to be, while they would enlist the services of beneficent deities.

Little or nothing is known of any festival occurring at the beginning of the second half of the winter season, i.e., on February 1st. We are better informed about the festival at the beginning of summer, Beltane, and the Midsummer festival. Readers should first of all clear their minds of any idea that Beltane or the name of the god Belenos (who is not known to have any connexion with Beltane) has anything to do with the Semitic Baal and his worship, which enthusiastic, well-intentioned, but erroneous, Celticists have believed to have been known and practised in this country, making use of a false etymology for this purpose. The Baal or Baals of the east were never worshipped here. Beltane is made up of two words, which together give the meaning of "bright fire," either with reference to the sun or to the bonfire which symbolized it. Belenos similarly means "splendid fire."

The bonfires were sometimes set alight on hills, and here again new fire was brought to the dwellings from them. The fire was health-giving, it symbolized and aided the sun going forth in his strength. As health-giving, cattle were driven through it, or more likely, between two fires, and were thus protected from disease. People danced sunwise round the fire and ran sunwise round the fields with burning brands by way of stimulating growth in these. Survivals of the Beltane customs suggest that an animal or even a human victim was sacrificed in the fire. The bonfire represented and stimulated the sun then beginning to recover from its winter defeat and to renew its course with greater energy for its effect upon the earth's growth. There were ceremonies with "Beltane cakes," these being rolled down a slope, figuring the sun rolling through the heavens, and magically stimulating its action. There were other ceremonies in which water and sacred wells figured. These were meant to ensure a good rainfall, without which the earth's growth is impossible. We do not know precisely what part the May-king and May-queen played at Beltane, though these, and especially the latter, long survived in folk-custom. They, or their union, may have been meant to aid fertility, especially if, as is possible, they symbolized or were regarded as incarnations of vegetation spirits. The greater part played by the May Queen, as is seen in survivals of the custom, points to the more primitive aspects of fertility rites, possibly even to the place of a Mother or Earth-goddess.

The Midsummer festival was known all over Europe, and outside Celtic regions, nor did it differ essentially from Beltane. The bonfire and its adjuncts were conspicuous, and here again there is evidence of earlier animal or human sacrifices. A wheel or circle has from early times been a symbol of the sun. To set it rolling was to imitate the sun's course and by imitating to strengthen it. Hence a wheel, while burning, was rolled down a slope or through the fields, which benefited by this action. A tree had an important place in Beltane and Midsummer ceremonies, for in primitive belief, trees were the abodes of tree-spirits, which influence vegetation. The tree was borne. through fields and by dwellings, which benefited by this action The tree was then burned. Much that is explanatory of these customs, drawn from widespread sources, and stressing the importance of fertility, will be found in the volumes of Sir James Frazer's *The Golden Bough*, which should be consulted for further details and for the light which its distinguished writer has thrown upon fertility ceremonies and cults.

Lugnasadh fell on August 1st, which later became the Christian feast of Lammas. The name exists in different branches of the Celtic tongue, and there is general agreement that it was connected with the god Lug or Lugus, whose epithet *samildanach* is equivalent to Cæsar's for the Gaulish Mercury, "inventor of all arts." Lug seems, therefore, to have been a Celtic Mercury, a culture god rather than a sun deity. The gathering in Ireland, which occurred at Lugnasadh, was held at Taillte, "all Ireland" meeting there, but this may be a grandiose phrase, for similar gatherings were held at other places in Ireland. As Lammas was associated with the early harvest, so Lugnasadh may have been primarily connected with that, but the gatherings had other aspects also, e.g., social; marriages were arranged and there was horse-racing. With some degree of probability a cult of Lugus has been inferred in Gaul, for the name of Lyons was formerly Lugudunum, "stronghold of Lugus." Here there was an assembly of all Gaul in honour of the emperor Augustus, but this may have been in honour of Lugus before the Roman conquest, and there would be similar gatherings in other places. Little is known of what occurred, but if Lugnasadh were a harvest feast it would naturally be an occasion of joy and feasting. Plenty of corn, fruit, milk, and fish followed upon its due observance.

All of these festival gatherings had a connexion with fertility cults, a more primitive ceremonial surviving in more elaborate festivals. Fertility cults were based primarily upon the worship of an earth-goddess, and may at first have been mainly observed by women. Later, a god took the place of a goddess, or was joined with her, and the observance was not confined to women. Connected with this was the celebration of rites in which the spirit of the corn was implicated. It is not impossible that a human being was slain in order that his flesh and blood might fertilize the earth. Some of the human sacrifices in which the Celts delighted may have at first been connected with such a rite. That the Celts had such agricultural ceremonies is certain, though as civilization among them advanced, these were given a wider scope, while the worship of other deities, e.g., war-gods, became prominent. Some relics of the earlier stage survived locally, and these we may see in statements made by some classical writers, though how far they can be trusted is doubtful. They based their statements on hearsay, rather than on personal observation, and had a passion for equating deities and ceremonies of which they had heard, or which had perhaps come under their notice, with others familiar to them elsewhere. Pliny reports that, in Britain, in certain rites, married and unmarried women stained themselves with woad and were naked. Why they did this is not told, but elsewhere nudity in agricultural rites was essential. Strabo speaks of an island near Britain in which sacrifices were offered to goddesses whom he calls Demeter and Kore, but does not give their native names. Obviously, they were deities more or less like Demeter and Kore. The worship resembled that of the earth-goddess at Samothrace, and was thus directed to the purpose of fertility. Perhaps Strabo is reporting a similar worship of a god whom he calls Dionysius, practised by women of the Namnite group (those of Nantes) on an island at the mouth of the Loire. No man was allowed on the island. Once a year the temple, which must have been of a primitive kind, was unroofed and re-roofed on the same day. Each woman carried the materials for re-roofing, and if one dropped her load she was torn in pieces, which, with much clamour, were carried round the temple. Another writer, Dionysius Periegetes, says that the women were crowned with ivy. What god, or goddess, is intended by the reference to Dionysius, is not known, but we may connect the ceremony with fertility rites. These classical writers were content to give somewhat obscure notices, without attempting to explain them or, as it were, set them in their true context.

PLACES OF WORSHIP

Early medieval books of regulations regarding conduct show that some survivals of pagan belief and custom held sway over the people. One of these states the fines to be paid by those who made votive offerings to fountains, trees, or groves (*lucos*). Another, the *Indiculus superstitionum*, gives the Celtic name for such groves, *nimidos*. This stands for *nemeta*, plural of *nemeton*, a sacred or consecrated place or grove. In old Irish this occurs as *nemed*, and *firnemed* meant "a sacred grove." A name in Noricum is Tasinemetum, the grove of the god Tasis, a local diety, otherwise unknown.

There is little doubt that the earliest places of worship among the Celts were groves, some of which remained sacred after temples were built. In these would be a symbol or image of the god worshipped there, and an altar. Andrasta, the war goddess of the Iceni, had a grove in which were sacrificed victims of their victory over the Romans. Woods or groves in Anglesey, in which rites of worship had been celebrated and human sacrifices offered, on altars wet with the victims' blood, were destroyed by the Romans. Lucan gives a startling picture, much elaborated, with a poet's exaggeration, of a sacred grove and its "cruel altars," close to Massilia (Marseilles), which goes far to contradict ideas about the high culture and philosophy of the Druids. The leaves of the trees moved even when there was no wind to stir them. Birds would not mate in them and beasts avoided the grove. Misshapen trunks of trees served as images of deities, and they were covered with the blood of sacrificial victims. In this grove were altars, heaped with horrible offerings. He then goes on to speak of certain wonders of this grove, obviously popular superstitious beliefs about it. Great serpents encircled the trees. Trees themselves, like the burning bush which Moses saw, were wrapped in flames but not consumed. The earth was heard to groan. Dead trees revived. Considering these things, it is little wonder that this grove was approached in fear and trembling. Even the priest avoided it at midday and midnight, popular hours of dread, lest he should encounter the divine lord of the grove. From such a description, poetic and exaggerated as it is, we can understand the sanctity of the sacred *nemeton*, and why popular thought still venerated or feared such places in Christian times.

A Latin scholiast on this passage of Lucan's says that the Druids worship the gods in woods without temples. But were there no temples in the sense of buildings? Cæsar speaks of the "consecrated place" where the Druids met yearly, and of "consecrated places" where the spoils of victory were piled up, probably devoted to the gods. These might be groves or they might be temples of a simple kind and their sacred surroundings. In referring to the latter custom Diodorus speaks of "temples and the sacred precincts," as being the depositories of gold as an offering to the gods. Probably there were temples as well as groves. Thus Pliny speaks of a temple of the Boii which was most sacred to them and in which sacred things were preserved. Polybius also speaks of a temple of the Insubri in cisalpine Gaul. Plutarch talks of a temple in which the Arverni had hung Cæsar's sword, which, when he afterwards saw it and was advised to remove it, he allowed to remain, for he looked upon it as consecrated.

Few as the references to temples among the Gauls are in pre-Roman times, they show that they did exist, but could only have been of a simple kind, of wood rather than of stone. We have no description of them such as we have for some Scandinavian temples (p. 141). But when the Gauls were conquered and their native religion assimilated to that of Rome, they vied with their conquerors in erecting temples. These were for their own deities, whether equated or not with those of Rome, as many inscriptions by worshippers show. Their architecture was similar to that of the Roman temples. In them stood the images of the gods to whom the temples were dedicated. Worshippers who had been cured at sacred springs sometimes erected small temples where the springs issued, commemorating their gratitude in an inscription addressed to the deity of the spring. Thus at Aix-les-Bains, where there were hot springs, there is one telling how Licinius Rusus performed his vow to the presiding deity in this place, Bormo, equated with Apollo.

Of what form the native altars were, we have no means of knowing. In Ireland they were adorned with emblems. But generally they would be of a rude kind, a block of stone or a heap of stones. On these the victims were offered, or offerings were piled. Or again they were smeared with the victims' blood. As temples resembling those of the Romans succeeded the native temples, so many altars of Roman type were erected. and adorned these. From them are derived many of the inscriptions, telling to whom the altars were dedicated, with the name of the grateful donor. Some are carved and show figures of deities or scenes which have given much material to speculative enquirers, bent on explaining their meaning.

Though it has been claimed that the Druids were priests of a pre-Celtic people, accepted by the Celts, and that they were opposed to images of deities, there is no real evidence for this, and there is no reason to doubt that the Celts had images, of a simple or even rude form. Lucan speaks of shapeless trunks of trees in the grove at Massilia which served as images, of a primitive kind, doubtless typical of those in other places, e.g., the oak which was the symbol of the Celtic Zeus, spoken of by Maximus of Tyre, possibly roughly carved to represent the deity. Cæsar speaks of "many *simulacra*" or representations of the Gaulish Mercury. Were these actual images or, more likely, boundary stones like the Roman *lapides terminales* or the Greek *hermai*? Such stones might be rudely carved into a likeness of the human form. The Irish Celts had images like those of Cenn Cruaich and his satellites, ornamented with gold and silver, but these again may have been only rudely carved stones. For Britain there is no evidence, except that Gildas (sixth century) describes images there, with stiff and deformed features, mouldering in the ruined temples, but these were most likely images and temples of the time of the Roman occupation.

With the overpowering influence of Roman culture in Gaul and Britain, as temples on the Roman model were erected, so images of deities, both native and Roman, were set up, the latter often with a native name attached. Of some of these images still existing, e.g., of the three-headed deity, or of a crouching deity, or others, the art is crude and the images lack grace. They may, therefore, be pre-Roman, or have been fashioned on the model of earlier images.

The lives of saints in Gaul sometimes describe the destruction of images by Christian missionaries. This is also spoken of by St. Martin of Tours.

Some of the existing images bear symbols which refer presumably to their functions, like the wheel of the sun god.

CHAPTER IX

THE PRIESTHOOD

THE Celts had priests, generally known as Druids. There is a vague knowledge of these in the popular mind, partly drawn from what Pliny says of the ceremonial cutting of mistletoe from the oak by Druids, partly from the supposed connexion of the Druids with stone-circles, "Druidical circles," and other megalithic remains, a belief due mainly to the antiquary William Stukely, in the eighteenth century, known then as "The Arch-Druid." The Druids had nothing to do with these; they existed before their time; and similar monuments are found in parts of the world where Celts and Druids never lived.

As to the Druids and the mistletoe, this has been impressed on the mind from school-books, and exaggerated beyond all true value.

Among ancient writers there was a curious belief that philosophy had arisen among the barbarians and their priests, of whom the Druids were cited as an example. This was undoubtedly because there was a vague knowledge that the Druids were teachers, unlike most pagan priesthoods.

The earliest reference to the Druids is in passages of Sotion and pseudo-Aristotle preserved by Diodorus, that among the Celts and Galatae are Druids and Semnotheoi. But the fullest account of them comes from Cæsar, though it is by no means certain that all he wrote is correct. There is no reason to connect the word Druid with the oak, Greek *drus*, as Pliny does. The generally accepted derivation is that of Thurneysen that the name is a Latinized form of a native word *druida*, from *dru*, an intensive syllable, and *vid*, "to see," or "to know." The Druid was he whose outlook on the world or whose knowledge was greater than other men's. This need not imply that the knowledge was profound, as some classical writers thought, regarding the Druids as philosophers. Rather does the name and its derivation suggest the superior knowledge of him who has to do with the affairs of religion, and it might be applied equally to the shaman or medicine-man of other races.

We shall first look at Cæsar's account of the Druids. He begins by saying that, in Gaul, there are two classes of men of standing, the Druids and the *equites*, the common people being little thought of. The Druids are concerned with divine things, sacrifices, public and private, and the interpretation of religious matters. Many young men go to them for teaching and honour them. They decide in most disputes, public and private. In matters of crime, murder, inheritance, boundaries, they settle matters and appoint rewards and punishments. If any person or group of persons does not accept their decision, they interdict them from the sacrifices, a very grave penalty. Such men are regarded as impious and scoundrels, all men avoid them and shun their approach and talk, lest they should receive harm from contact with them. To those of them who seek it no justice is done, no honour is imparted.

Of all the Druids there is one who is chief and has the highest authority. When he dies, either one who excels in dignity succeeds, or, if there are several of such, the position is settled by the vote of the Druids, or the candidates even fight for it.

At a certain period of the year the Druids meet at a consecrated place in the region of the Carnutes, supposed to be the centre of all Gaul. Here come all who have disputes and submit to their decrees and judgments.

It is thought that the *disciplina* of the Druids was devised in Britain, and brought thence to Gaul, and at the present time those who wish to study it more diligently often go thither.

The Druids hold aloof from war nor do they pay tribute towards it. From all this they are freed, hence, tempted by these exemptions, many young men of their own will go to receive training from them or are sent to them by parents and relations. They are said to learn a great number of verses, and some remain for twenty years in this training. The Druids do not think it fitting to commit these verses to writing, but in most other matters, in public and private business, they use

Greek letters. This, as Cæsar thinks, is done for two reasons—
they do not wish the training to become common, and they
who learn are not to rely on writing and forsake the exercise of
the memory.

In the main, the Druids desire to persuade men that souls
do not die, but after death pass from one to another. And this
they think will chiefly excite to courage by putting away the
fear of death.

The Druids also discuss and teach to the youths many
things about the stars and their movements, about the size of
the universe and this world, about the nature of things, about
the force and power of the immortal gods.

When writing about sacrifices Cæsar says that those who
offer these employ the Druids to carry them out. The supposed
descent of the Gauls from the Celtic Dispater is also said to
have been taught by the Druids.

It is obvious from Cæsar's words that the Druids had great
power. Apart from their position as priests, they acted as
judges, settled disputes, and appointed rewards and punishments. Those who did not submit to their decisions were
ostracized and were not allowed to take part in religious
ceremonies. This was based on the view that the gods looked
with disfavour on all actions which questioned their rule.
Offenders must be shut off from the privilege of worship as
well as from social intercourse, as enemies of the gods and of
society. Certain criminals were sacrificed in order to win the
favour of the gods, who would be displeased at their conduct
and might visit their displeasure on the community. Apparently
the Druids had the power of electing rulers, for in another part
of his book Cæsar tells how he accepted the appointment of
Convictolitavis to supreme authority among the Aedui, he
having been elected by the priests, as was customary at certain
times. In Ireland there is some evidence of Druids there
interfering in the election of a chief king.

The supremacy of one Druid over all others is found also in
Ireland, where the chief Druid is called in the Latin life of
St. Patrick *primus magus*.

The annual assembly in a consecrated place where the
Druids judged and settled disputes is not known from any other

source, but Strabo says that being considered the most just of men, the Druids were entrusted with decisions both in public and private affairs. Formerly they had been arbiters in affairs of war, and made the opponents stop even when lined up in order of battle. So Diodorus Siculus speaks of the obedience paid to them both in peace and war, and this obedience was given even by those hostile to them. The Druids would step forward even when the opposing bodies had their weapons ready for combat, and cause them to cease as if a spell had been cast upon wild beasts. Perhaps their desire was to put an end to tribal wars.

The training given by the Druids to those who went to them as pupils, lasted for twenty years, almost certainly an exaggeration, though for those who wished to become Druids there would be stages of initiation. The instruction was oral and conveyed in verse, and was not committed to writing. It is a mistake to suppose that it included philosophy of an exalted kind, as we shall see. The verses would include traditional history, sagas, myths. As to committing them to memory and their not being written down, there is a parallel in the ancient Hindu books, copious as they were. They were memorized, memory was considered a better vehicle than manuscript. For as Cæsar comments on the Druidic use of memory in teaching, writing is bad for the student's diligence and for the memory, or, as Montaigne said, "what I place on paper I dismiss from my memory." To write down the contents of the Hindu sacred books was regarded as a terrible crime. These views were held by the Druids. The main subjects of this teaching, according to Cæsar, were astronomy, perhaps more of the nature of astrology, the size of the universe, the order of nature, mythical accounts of the origin of things, cosmogonic myths such as are common to all races. Mela also speaks of their professing to know the size and form of the earth, the movements of the heavens and of the stars. The likeness of his words to Cæsar's suggests that they are using a common source, probably Poseidonius. There was teaching also about the deities, of which Cæsar gives an example when he speaks of the Celtic Dis, myths about them and their functions. Diogenes Laertius speaks of the Druids' moral teaching set forth, to judge from the example he gives, in maxims—"To honour the gods, to do no evil, to be brave." At a later period Pliny describes the Druids as "a sort of prophets and doctors." But from examples given by him their medical knowledge was rather magical, a kind of plant-lore, of the magico-medicinal use of herbs. In connexion with religious matters, they taught the immortality of the soul or rather a future bodily life, not merely a spirit or shadow life after death. This particular teaching of theirs the Druids held to be powerful in overcoming the fear of death, and so inciting to courage. More will be said of this, especially about Cæsar's words as pointing to a belief in transmigration, in a later chapter.

There were name-giving rites in which a Druid named a child, e.g., from some particular event which had happened at or near the time of birth, a widespread custom with many peoples. Some notices in Irish and Welsh literature show that a kind of lustration was used by the Druids, later called "heathen baptism." A Druid also cast a horoscope or took omens from the heavens.

There was a vague belief in the ancient world that the Druids were philosophers of a lofty kind, and that they taught the doctrine of Pythagoras about the migration of the soul after death. This is asserted by Diodorus, whose words again resemble Cæsar's save that the latter does not mention Pythagoras, and again both may be quoting Poseidonius. He says that the belief of Pythagoras is held by them that souls are immortal and after a number of years begin a new life, the soul entering another body. Valerius Maximus, referring to the belief of the Gauls in immortality, says, "I would call them fools (for this), but that these breech-wearing folk hold what the mantle-wearing Pythagoras taught." Ammianus Marcellinus also connects the Gaulish belief with the Pythagorean doctrine. Clement of Alexandria speaks of the Celtic philosophers, the Druids, and Origen says that a disciple of Pythagoras, Zamolxis, in the fifth century B.C., had taught Pythagorean doctrines among the Gauls.

There was a tendency among classical writers to regard the Druids as philosophers, thus Diodorus says that among the Gauls "are philosophers, as we may call them, men learned in religious affairs, who are honoured among them, and are called Druids." Strabo also speaks of the Druids studying natural philosophy.

These are the statements of men who had no first-hand knowledge of the Druids, and some of whom like Clement and Origen wrote long after the Druids had ceased. The "philosophy" of the Druids could have been of a simple kind only: it was never brought to light, nor, apart from the vague references to it, had it any effect on classical thought. Druids in the south of Gaul may have come under the influence of learning among Greek colonies there, e.g., at Marseilles, but such influence did not extend far, though it may explain what Cæsar says of the use of Greek letters in what they committed to writing, whether public or private affairs. Among Druids of a higher type might be counted Diviciacus, of the Aedui, who had great weight with that tribe and was held in respect by Cæsar. He was known to Cicero, who speaks of his professing to know the order of nature, yet he used divination about future events.

The belief in the Druids as philosophers is largely discounted by their connexion with human sacrifice, and by a more intimate knowledge of them. Mela speaks of the savagery of the sacrifices. Suetonius calls the religion of the Druids among the Gauls one of detestable cruelty. The practical Romans were aware of this. In 97 B.C. the Senate had interdicted human sacrifice throughout the Empire, and when Gaul became part of the Empire it came under the effect of this law. But special measures were taken against cruel rites. Augustus had already prohibited the religion of the Druids "of dire cruelty," to Gauls who were Roman citizens. Before A.D. 37 the Senate, at the instance of Tiberius, suppressed the Druids. Claudius (A.D. 41–54) completely abolished their religion. These laws probably meant an abolition of human sacrifices and of magic, "crimes and notorious superstitions" are what Aurelius Victor says were abolished. Strabo, at an earlier time, speaks of Druidic customs being suppressed as well as all things pertaining to sacrifice and divination and opposed to "our usages." Mela says that sacrifices were still offered symbolically, by drawing blood from the victim. The Druids, as such, did not disappear, but their powers were vastly restricted, e.g., in political matters.

Rome could permit no rival here. Schools in Gaul were established by the Romans, which, as early as A.D. 21, attracted those who could have gone for instruction to the Druids. The existence of Druids in Gaul in the fourth century is attested by Ausonius, who speaks of two of these attached to the temple of Belenos.

In Gaul, as in Roman Britain, the Druids as a class, certainly their power, waned before the mingling of the native religion with that of Rome, and also with the introduction of Chris-tianity. We have a glimpse of Druidic power in Britain, before the Romans became masters there, in what Tacitus tells of them in Anglesey, their altars, groves, and human sacrifices. Yet on the death of the Emperor Vitellius in A.D. 69, whose troops had burned the Capitol, and the subsequent confusion in Roman affairs, there was a belief in Gaul that the Empire was ending. The Druids were at this time strong enough to utter prophecies to this effect.

Beyond the Roman pale Druids remained strong. In lives of saints we find them opposed in Scotland by Christian mis-sionaries, e.g., St. Columba, just as they were in Ireland, where St. Patrick's hymn seeks defence against the spells of Druids.

There is reference on four inscriptions and in the Latin writer Hirtius to priests known as *gutuatros*, a word meaning "speaker," one who invokes the gods. Judging by the inscriptions a *gutuatros* seems to have been attached to the temple of a god. Elaborate theories have been built upon these few and obscure references. We may see in these *gutuatri* merely a class of Druids, just as in all probability the bards and diviners were special branches of the Druidic priesthood.

Some of the functions of the Druids in Gaul are ascribed also to Irish Druids. According to one account Irish Kings were elected by them. They held an important place in the royal court, and in matters of gravity the King kept silence until the Druid had spoken. We hear little of their connexion with sacri-fices in Ireland, but not much is said of sacrifice in the texts, and there are occasional references to the Druids' part in these. Their teachings are mentioned. They taught the knowledge of

Druidism (*druidecht*), and among their pupils were the daughters of Kings as well as the mythical heroes of the past. The Irish Druids are not spoken of in the texts as priests, rather as magicians, and some have held that this was their true character. This, however, may be due to deliberate suppression, on the part of Christian scribes and annalists, of much that pertained to the earlier paganism. On the other hand, it has been maintained that many references to the power of Irish Druids are due to a medieval romantic desire to assimilate them to the Druids of Gaul as described in classical writers. While it may be true that some of the functions ascribed to them are imaginary, there is no reason to believe that the Goidels of Ireland had no priests, but magicians only. True, it is their magic which is stressed in the tales. In all things, especially war, they aided their people by magic. Such magic became mythical and even the Tuatha Dé Danann are said to have been taught it by them, e.g., power over nature, blinding snowstorms, clouds of fire, torrents of water, spreading the sea over a plain. They could transform themselves into the likeness of others, or produce a magic mist which made men invisible, or caused oblivion. The *airbe druad* was a magic hedge cast round an armed force, which opponents could not break through. They restored the dead to life. These fabled magic deeds show how, in popular belief, the powers of actual Druids were unbounded. Hence, they are called *magi* in the lives of saints, whose alleged powers equalled their own. But it should be remembered that Pliny, who describes some of the Druidic priestly arts, also calls them *magi, Druidae, ita suos appellant magos*, and then also uses the word "priest," *sacerdos*, of the one who cut the mistletoe.

Bards among the Celts are mentioned by Poseidonius. Diodorus and Strabo speak of bards and poets whose songs, composed by themselves, might be either of praise or obloquy. They sang to the accompaniment of instruments like lyres, and were often attached to the train of chiefs. In Ireland and in Wales there were also bards, who in both countries had a high place, though in the former country there was a distinction between the bard and the *file* or poet, who had a higher position than the bard and a long period of training.

Both Diodorus and Strabo speak of a third class, the diviners, the former using the Greek word *mantis*, the latter *vates*. They were held in high respect, and foretold the future by the flight of birds and the slaughter of sacred animals. Strabo calls them natural philosophers. The multitude were subservient to them. They investigated sublime things, according to Ammianus Marcellinus, and explained the secret things of nature. In Ireland there were also diviners. But Druids themselves were diviners, and it is possible that there was a connexion between all three groups, and that bards and diviners were branches of the Druids proper. In Ireland the power of the bards was great and they were feared for their powers of satire which is said to have caused disfigurement to the face or even death. They preserved in their verses all that was important—traditional history, laws, genealogies, and the like.

In later Roman writers of the third century there are a few references to women called *dryades*. They were soothsayers, and predicted the future to Alexander Severus and Diocletian, and they were consulted by Aurelian. They need not be regarded as "Druidesses," though there were women attached to certain shrines, e.g., a *flaminica sacerdos* of a goddess Thucolis at Le Prugnon, and an *antistita deae* at Arles. In Ireland there were female diviners, *ban-fáthi, ban-filid*, and the name *ban-drui* is sometimes attached to the latter.

Basing their opinion on Cæsar's words, "it is thought that the *disciplina* of the Druids was found in Britain and thence passed to Gaul," as well as on other grounds, some have held that this expresses a fact, whereas Cæsar's words are a mere opinion. One view, that of M. D'Arbois de Jubainville, is that Druids were priests of the Goidels in Britain, and that when they were conquered by the Gauls, their priests, the Druids, imposed their domination upon the conquerors, and became their priests, and also those of the Gauls in Gaul. This assumes that there were Goidels in Britain, 300 to 200 B.C. But were they there? We do not know certainly that they were the earliest Celtic inhabitants of Britain, indeed it is believed that there were no Goidels in Britain at that time. The theory assumes that the Gauls were a priestless people, which is unlikely.

Others insist that the Druids were priests of pre-Celtic people, not Goidels, and that the Celts accepted them as their priests. There is no substantial evidence for this, and from all classical notices the Druids appear as themselves Celts and as the dominant priesthood of Celts. One argument is that human sacrifice, magic, and the like were opposed to "Aryan" sentiment. If so, why did the Gauls so willingly accept these? "Aryans" were indeed no less barbarous than the non-Aryans whom they conquered. Everything goes to show that the Druids were the native Celtic priesthood. It is unlikely that they came to Gaul from Britain, which was less civilized even than Gaul, and if it were true, as Cæsar says, that those who wished to study Druidic affairs more closely went to Britain for this purpose, it can only mean that Druids there were more highly thought of. But again this is merely an opinion, his own or some other person's, given by Cæsar.

The "system of Druidism" is sometimes spoken of as if it were a separate entity, outside Celtdom. Actually it was the religion of the Celts, the priests of which were Druids.

CHAPTER X

THE POWERS OF MAGIC

IN all parts of the world a belief in magic has existed, and it was supposed to be possessed by certain classes of people. But to some degree anyone might practise it, and it was sometimes ascribed specially to women, just as in later times it was mostly women as witches who claimed or were believed to possess magical powers, and were in league with the devil. It is possible that women were the chief magic wielders among the earlier Celts and that some of them still retained such powers even after the Druids came to be regarded as the chief magic wielders. Pomponius Mela describes the actions of nine "priestesses" (*antistites*) on an island off Brittany remarkable as the oracle of a Gaulish deity. They lived in perpetual virginity and wielded power over sea and wind by reciting charms. They were able to heal those deemed incurable. They knew the future and predicted it, but only to sailors who consulted them before setting out on a voyage. It was said of them that they could assume whatever animal forms they pleased. The truth of this has been contested, but we may take it as it stands, and in much later times these were the powers ascribed to witches. The so-called Dryades in the third century had powers of prediction and divination, and foretold their future to Emperors, as the witches did to Macbeth (p. 74).

Pliny speaks of the Druids as *magi*, and as "that race of prophets and doctors." This shows that they were regarded as magicians and foretold the future. But what of their medical and healing powers? Pliny himself shows that these were connected with magic. In the famous mistletoe rite, this plant and the tree on which it grows were held to be sacred, the mistletoe being rarely found. It was culled on the sixth day of the moon. Sacrifice was offered and a feast held. Two white bulls were brought to the place. A white-robed Druid ascended the tree and cut the mistletoe with a golden sickle. It was caught in a white cloth, the animals were sacrificed, and prayer was offered for the deity's blessing on this gift of mistletoe, the "all-healer." It was a remedy against poison, and a potion made of it caused animals to be fruitful. Thus the mistletoe was used in a magico-medical manner, whatever the original purpose of the ceremony may have been. Another plant, *samolus*, was gathered by a person fasting, with the left hand, and it required to be completely uprooted. The person gathering it must not look back. It was used to heal disease in cattle. Another plant, *selago*, was cut by a person dressed in white, and with feet bare and washed. The Druids said that it preserved from accident and its smoke, when burned, was wholesome for eye trouble.

Whether the Celts were more open to magical beliefs than other races is questionable, but the idea of magic had much influence over their minds, and enormous powers of magic were freely fathered not only on Druids but on deities, heroes, and others in Irish literature as well as in Welsh, whatever may have been true of Gaul. The facts told of them are extraordinary. We move in an atmosphere of magic in which, as is obvious, belief is expected. The deities appear more as mighty magicians than as gods. Yet so much greater was the magic of the Druids that the gods were said to have learned it from them, or at least from four great Druids. Some of these magical feats have already been mentioned. Shape-shifting was common to deities and Druids. They could change their own forms and those of others, and no incident is more common than this. To become invisible, to make others invisible, was a frequent magic act. Other actions depended upon particular potions being administered, e.g., causing forgetfulness, or the magic or Druidic sleep, a sleep which made the sleeper motionless, or in which he revealed what was hidden in his mind. This points to some kind of hypnotic action, and suggestion and hypnotism are known to have been practised by shamans, medicine-men, and magicians among savage and barbaric peoples, as may be found in some of the volumes issued by the Bureau of Ethnology of the Smithsonian Institute of America. There is thus no reason why these should not have been used by the Druids.

People were "rhymed" to death both by Druids and *filid*, an action of frequent occurrence in Irish texts. The "rhyme"

was a satire or spell spoken against a person, and it was believed
by him to have great power of evil, and in consequence he
succumbed to it and frequently died. A primitive kind of magic
is found in that of saying a spell over a spear and then casting
it into the shadow of the proposed victim, so that he died.

The spell had powerful effects, as the spoken word weighted
both with the name of a deity or with an appeal to him to
perform the act specified in the spell, has had a universal
vogue. There are, or were recently, poetical spells current in
the West Highlands in which the appeal is to our Lord or to a
saint to perform some act of healing. With few differences save
the substitution of the name of a pagan deity, similar spells or
charms existed among the Babylonian and other races. The Irish
file had to learn many spells by which, as well as the methods of
repeating them, certain effects upon those against whom they
were spoken would follow.

To show the general belief in the power of magic among the
Goidels of Ireland, there is proof that similar powers were
ascribed to early Christian missionaries there, who, if their
biographers are to be credited, met the magic acts of Druids
with similar and greater powers than their own, thus reducing
them to impotence.

Amulets were used to counteract or ward off disease and
other evils. Little models of a horse with a ring for suspension
have been frequently found, representing the goddess Epona,
and they would be worn as a means of gaining her protection.
Other small models of divine animals—the bull, the boar—
were carried for a like purpose. Similarly there exist numerous
little wheels, which if they are symbols of the god with the
wheel, the sun-god, may be regarded as helpful to the wearer.
Pliny speaks of the powers ascribed to coral by *aruspices* and
vates for averting perils, and says that the Gauls adorned their
swords, shields, and helmets with it. As a protective it was
bound on infants. It was used against stomachic and urinary
troubles, the coral being reduced to powder by fire, mixed
with water and swallowed. Another amulet mentioned by
Pliny is the "serpent's egg." This was produced by serpents
interlaced from their spume and foam, and was tossed by them
into the air. If anyone was fortunate enough to catch it ere it

fell he had at once to put running water between himself and the reptiles. As seen by Pliny and described by him, it may have been a fossil echinus, such as has been found in tombs in Gaul. It was believed to bring success to its owner in a lawsuit or in gaining access to kings. A Roman citizen who had brought this amulet into court was put to death in the reign of Claudian.

CHAPTER XI

THE FUTURE LIFE

Cæsar said that a tradition of the Druids, held by the Gauls, was that they were descended from one father, Dis, an underworld god, whose native name he does not give. This earth or under earth deity must have been a god of fertility, for all growing things have their roots under the earth's surface. From this underworld region men had come forth to people the earth. Other races had similar myths of human beginnings.

Like other peoples, the Celts believed it necessary to provide the dead with grave-goods—utensils, ornaments, weapons—for their use in the future life. There were even human sacrifices at graves, for the dead must still have their slaves, their wives, and children, beyond the grave. Cæsar speaks of the costly funerals of the Gauls, at least those of high rank, and says that all which was thought to be dear to the dead was burned on the pyre, even animals. Shortly before he wrote wives and dependants dear to the departed were burnt with them. All this shows that the Celts, like most other races, had definite beliefs in existence after death. As far as the Irish Goidels are concerned there is further proof in this that some passages in the texts speak of providing the dead with all that was necessary in the life beyond. Now these customs wherever found point to a belief that the dead lived on in the grave. Hence also the custom of putting sacrificial food on the grave. There is some evidence also of consulting the dead at their graves, as if they were alive there, both in Irish texts and in classical testimony. Moreover Celtic folk-lore seems to bear witness to such primitive beliefs. If the dead reappear they seem not to be spirits only, but of substantial form. Such ideas persisted long after the actual belief had faded, or were still held along with other beliefs about the dead, as we shall see also among the Scandinavians. The underworld of the dead was merely an extension of the grave as the dead man's home. The grave itself was a constricted underworld. Where there were many graves together such an underworld became more spacious. This gave rise to the belief in a wide, hollow, underworld region where the dead lived on, conceived, though not always, as an abode of shades, like the Roman place of the *manes*, the Babylonian Aralu—"the land without return," the Hebrew Sheol as envisaged in some passages of the Old Testament. Other beliefs existed, e.g., in another world of the dead, far off, but not underground nor in the sky. Sometimes all such beliefs were held simultaneously, apparently without any sense of incongruity.

With some peoples the underworld was not gloomy, not an abode of shades. This seems to have been true of the Celts. Otherwise it is difficult to explain the apparent astonishment of Roman observers, accustomed to their own cheerless belief in the underworld of mere shades, when they came in contact with a belief in a more exuberant life after death. This is seen first in what Cæsar says, "Chiefly the Druids teach that souls do not die, but pass from one to another after death. This they think excites to valour, the fear of death being neglected." Cæsar does not refer here to a transmigration belief, the soul passing to a new bodily life on earth, but to the soul's being clad, as it were, with a new body in the other world, though he does not say where that is supposed to be.

Cæsar's testimony is confirmed by that of Lucan (A.D. 39 to 65). Of the Druids he says, "From you we learn that the bourne of man's life is not the silent halls of Erebus (not that of the shadowy *manes*), but the spirit animates the members in another world (or region). If your songs are true, death is but the centre of a long life." Hence, he adds, the fear of death was unknown to the Celtic warrior. It would be cowardly to take care of a life which will be his again. There is a kind of wistful admiration in Lucan's testimony, as if he wished that he himself could share this belief.

Both Cæsar and Lucan bear witness to a bodily, not spirit, immortality. The soul will be furnished with bodily members. Diodorus Siculus confirms this belief in a bodily life after death, though he connects it with the opinions of Pythagoras. Souls are immortal, and after a certain term of years begin a new life, the soul entering into another body. The Pythagorean doctrine was that souls entered new bodies, animal or human, as an expiation for guilt in their previous existence. Diodorus makes no reference to this. What seems to have struck him, as it did Cæsar and Lucan, was the Celtic belief in a bodily existence after death. Hence he found a link of connexion with the Pythagorean belief about the soul passing into another body on earth. In no way could the Pythagorean doctrine of transmigration if held by the Celts, be compatible with what he adds about their custom, which he says is consequent upon the Celtic belief in bodily existence after death—"at funerals some throw letters written to their dead relatives on the funeral pyre," as if the dead would be able to read them.

Similarly Valerius Maximus speaks of the Celtic belief in immortality and its consequence, viz., that debts would be repaid in the next world (*apud inferos*). This belief he would find incredible if it were not that of Pythagoras. Pomponius Mela speaks of Druidic teaching that souls are immortal and that there is another life with the *manes* (Lucan's *orbis alius*). Hence they consume with fire or bury things suitable to them as when living. Formerly affairs of business and exaction of a loan were transferred to the after life (*ad inferos*), and there were those who threw themselves freely on the pyres of their relatives. Ammianus Marcellinus, quoting Timagenes, speaks of the immortality of the soul taught by the Druids.

This idea of a vigorous life of a bodily kind assured to souls in the other world had obviously struck the classical observers as a strange, almost incredible, belief. Had they recalled the happy other world allotted to the heroes of Troy by Zeus in a region at the ends of the earth, the islands of the blest, where Kronos reigned, as described by Hesiod, their wonder might have been less.

Where was this other world of the Celts situated, Lucan's *orbis alius*? The words may denote another region of this world, and it was probably an underworld region. Some have connected it with the island Wonderland of the Irish Celts, to be considered in the next chapter, but this was emphatically not an abode of the dead, but of deities, supernatural beings, who might and sometimes did, invite favoured people, while still alive, never when dead, to visit them. In the underworld, ruled by a beneficent deity, the dead led a pleasant existence. They were not cheerless phantoms, dwelling in a shadowy, undesirable region, but souls endued with bodies, which enabled them to enjoy the blessings of the after life.

As the belief in transmigration of souls has been attributed to Druidic teaching, was there any known belief in this among the Celts? We have seen that it does not really underlie what the classical writers say of the Druids, and no myth from Gaul on this subject exists. It appears here and there in some myths of the insular Celts, but is there connected with deities and heroes, never with the mass of men. In some tales a deity has assumed some small animal form, an insect or a worm, and this, swallowed by a mortal woman, causes her to give birth to a personage who is the deity in more or less mortal form.

Transmigration, in the sense of a series of re-births, cannot be said to be clearly found in the mythical tales and is never connected with a future life. We have such utterances as that of the Irish Amairgen—"I am the bull of seven battles, I am the eagle on the rock, I am a boar for courage, etc." Does this mean that he had actually been re-born in these forms, or is he not merely claiming that he has effected a series of transformations? As we have seen, the Welsh Gwion, assuming several forms, finally that of a grain of wheat, is swallowed by Cerridwen in the form of a hen. She then gives birth in due time to Taliesin, who is thus a re-birth of Gwion. In a poem stated to be his, but of a date long after the pagan period, Taliesin boasts of the various forms which he had assumed or of the re-births of himself which he had caused. This throws no light on a general belief in re-birth. In Irish story Tuan Mac-Caraill had lived from the days of the first and during the later invasions of Ireland, and survived long enough to recount their story. How did this happen? As an aged man he had fallen asleep, and awoke to find himself a stag. He lived long in that form, and then became successively a boar, a hawk, a salmon. The salmon was eaten by the wife of Caraill, and Tuan was born of her. He was thus able to recollect his successive existences and tell them to St. Finnan.

In all such tales or mythical stories, there is no real transmigration of souls, such as Pythagoras taught. All that they show is a belief in successive transformations and in occasional re-birth. It is known that the soul has sometimes been supposed to have the form of a minute creature, and such a belief may lie behind the stories of re-births of beings who had taken the form of worm or insect.

A worship of ancestors may be inferred from a number of facts regarding the dead and from funeral usages. Apart from the practice of burying grave-goods with the dead, which is universal, there was a great costliness in sacrifices made at the rites of burial. Of this, Cæsar says, "All things thought to have been dear to the dead in their life-time are thrown into the fire, even animals, and not long ago servants and dependants who were considered dear to them were burned with them at the end of the funeral rites." This showed honour, if of a cruel kind, paid to the departed. Pomponius Mela corroborates this to some extent, for he speaks of burning and burying with the dead, things suitable for the living, while he adds that the human victims at the funeral rites were slaves whose own wish it was to continue with their masters in the new life, or persons slain to act as messengers to the dead. The latter custom resembles that of burning letters that these might be read by deceased relatives, as stated by Diodorus Siculus.

The tombs or *tumuli* (mounds) erected over the dead were sacred, and this may account for the fact that some of the greater ones, e.g., Brug na Boinne at New Grange, were associated with the Tuatha Dé Danann as the places whither they had retired after their defeat by the Milesians.

The gatherings in Ireland at sacred times had some connexion with the memory of the dead: they were held on the yearly memorial of the deaths of rulers. Tradition ascribed the origin of some of these festivals to a desire to do honour to the departed, e.g., Lug was said to have founded that of Lugnasadh in memory of Tailtiu. The dead were also commemorated at Samhain, the winter festival in November. The Christian festivals of All Saints and All Souls (November 1st and 2nd) began to be observed in the seventh and tenth centuries respectively, and in Celtic regions some aspects of the pagan festival still surviving were attached to these. Thus food is placed out for the dead at these times in Brittany, and this is doubtless an old custom surviving to which a Christian aspect has been given.

On the whole the evidence for ancestor worship among the Celts is scanty. We are forced to look for it mainly in survivals, the meaning of which is not always clear. There is the Highland custom of erecting a cairn, secretly, where a dead body has been found, a survival of the custom of erecting one over the dead generally. There are Irish and Breton customs of placing food out for the dead or inviting them to the funeral feast. The hearth was the place of the ancestors and offerings were made to them there. It survives as a sacred place in superstitions about the helpful spirit, whose domain it is, and who does work secretly, the ancestral spirit become a Brownie, Gruagach, *lutin*, and the like.

CHAPTER XII

THE WORLD AS REGARDED BY THE CELTS

How did the Celts look upon the world in which they lived? No Celtic myth of creation as a whole has survived, such as we find among the ancient Babylonians. There are references in Irish writings, and there are later folk survivals or folk-tales, which point to the belief that certain parts of nature had their origin in this or the other cause. Thus sacred wells, through careless encroachment or some other cause, overflowed, the spirit or deity of the well thus showing anger at such treatment of his or her domain. The result of the overflowing was the formation of a river, e.g., the Shannon or the Boyne, or a loch, as was told of Loch Neagh. Again the tears of a deity, such as those shed by the god Manannan when he died, produced three lochs. In his poem *Argonautica* Apollonius similarly says of the Celtic people that they tell how the eddies of the river Po are the copious tears which fell from Apollo, and were caused by his father's having thrust him from heaven to earth. This must be a Celtic myth, told of a deity who had been equated with Apollo.

As to human origins nothing is known save what is contained in Cæsar's statement about the Druidic tradition that men are descended from the Celtic god whom he calls Dis, an earth or under-earth deity. Whether this points to actual descent or to some myth, such as is found in other parts of the world, among South African tribes, in ancient Greece, in Peru, about men emerging from the earth, is not known.

There are some notices of beliefs which are of a primitive kind. Some peoples have thought that the sky was supported from the earth by one or more pillars or by a tree, or that it was easily reached from the top of a mountain. Such opinions are found in Japanese, in early Egyptian, in Hebrew, and in North Asiatic myths. Traces of similar beliefs occur in Celtic regions, suggesting that the Celts had myths of such a kind.

Thus St. Patrick and St. Brigit are compared to the two pillars of the world. This must have been borrowed from a myth about pillars which supported the earth or the sky. In later Irish literature there are descriptions of islands supported on pillars.

In one of the tales of the Cúchulainn saga it was said by his reputed father Sualtam that the alleged defeat of the hero was as improbable as that the heaven should crash, the sea empty itself, or the earth burst asunder. King Conchobar said, "Heaven is above us, the earth is under us, the sea surrounds us," and then added, "If the sky does not fall with its stars upon the earth, if the earth is not broken to pieces, if the desert of the sea does not come from its blue domain upon the earth," then he would recover the spoil taken by his enemies. If, in the words of Sualtam, these catastrophes are thought to be impossible, Conchobar apparently regards them as possible, though remote. Now, according to Strabo, the Druids taught that men's souls and the world were indestructible, though in the future fire and water would prevail over them. He also tells how certain Celts informed Alexander the Great that they feared one thing only, the fall of the sky upon their heads. It is thus possible, if uncertain, that there was a Celtic myth of a future catastrophe in which sky and earth would perish. If such a myth existed, there may be a reference to it in the words of the war-goddess Badb when, after the defeat of the Fomorians, she told this to "the royal heights," the waters, and the estuaries of Ireland—these being personified, and then she went on to utter a prophecy of the end of the world and of future ills. This may, however, be a Christian scribe's interpolation. But there are some likenesses in this possible Celtic belief of a destruction of the world to the Scandinavian myth of doom involving the world and the gods (p. 164).

CHAPTER XIII

A CELTIC WONDERLAND

T H E idea of an Elysium on earth, an earthly Paradise, an abode of deities and supernatural beings, but not a place of the dead, is not strictly a religious conception, though it has links with religious beliefs about the deities, and has romantic and idealistic aspects. It was well developed among the insular Celts, especially in Ireland, and is the subject of a number of mythical and romantic tales. How far a similar conception existed among the continental Celts is unknown, since their myths have not survived.

These stories of the Irish Celts are on the whole pre-Christian, though we owe their survival to Christian scribes who copied them, perhaps from earlier written sources, or more likely from oral tradition, and thus preserved them more or less intact. Here and there they may have retouched them in accordance with Christian belief, but it is remarkable how little this occurred. These tales certainly show an idealism which one would hardly have expected, and they have a parallel with the romantic tales and beliefs of ancient Greece.

The main idea of these tales is that a wonderful and beautiful region exists, full of splendid aspects of nature, rich in exquisite trees and bird-music, peaceful, untroubled by storms or earthly disasters, a place most desirable in every aspect. Here dwelt immortal beings, under the rule of a deity, usually one of those worshipped by mortals, Mannanan, Mider, and others. In these happy places death was unknown; there existed all that could be imagined or desired by mortals, all that might be dreamt of as possible by them. The main interest of the myths is that a mortal is invited or lured to share the delights of this happy state, usually by a goddess who appears to him. He departs, and if he returns to earth, it is sometimes to find that the supernatural lapse of time, a theme told in many different forms in all parts of the world, has happened. What seemed to him in the happy land only a short time has been in reality long as measured by time on earth. He returns to earth to find that those he knew there have long perished, "all his friends are lapped in lead."

This happy land has different names—Tir na n-Og, "the land of youth," Mag Mell "the pleasant plain," Tir na m-Beo, "the land of the living," Tir fa Tonn, "land under waves." Sometimes it is a mysterious island or one of several islands. Again it is underground or in one of the *síd* or mounds, or it is beneath the waters, or it may appear on earth's surface for a time, hidden by mist. Sometimes through conflation of ideas the *síd* Wonderland and the island Paradise are confused. But wherever situated, it is desirable. Why were mortals invited to it? Now by special favour of its divine inhabitants, or because a goddess had fallen in love with a mortal, or again, strange to say, to help the immortals against others who are their enemies. This seems to strike a jarring note in tales of a place described as full of peace and harmony. But there may have been two conceptions of this immortal land, one that of peaceful people, one that of warriors, and we know that there were myths of wars among the gods. Sometimes this immortal land is described as the dwelling of beautiful women, but then it is one of several islands.

The pleasing aspects of this land are described in the tales about it. It is a land of immortal beings, ever-living ones, of eternal youth. On the other hand this immortality may be the result of eating or drinking certain immortal substances. In one story the swine of the god Manannan are immortal, when slain they come alive again. With their flesh he is said to have made the Tuatha Dé Danann immortal. There was also the ale of the god Goibniu, which had similar virtues. Why should the immortal nature of the gods be dependent upon such things? Here we may see a transference of man's own experience of intoxicants. He is raised above himself, he thinks himself immortal. So he may have argued that the gods were made and kept immortal by special drinks, like the Greek nectar (see p. 115 for the Scandinavian apples of Idunn, conferring immortality on the gods). The food of the land was inexhaustible, moreover it had whatever taste its eater might prefer. In the tale called *Echtra Condla* an apple which a goddess gives to a mortal satisfies him for many days. Such fruits, as well as nuts or even rowan-berries, all doubtless of a particular kind, are said to be the food of the gods. Ideas such as these were not confined to the Celts, as many myths from other regions show.

A branch of one of the immortal trees of this Wonderland was sometimes used to attract a mortal thither. On it grew wonderful fruit. These trees themselves produced music such as was never heard on earth, and on them perched birds whose song was full of all allurements. Even the stones were magical. One stone swelled with choruses of hundreds, "sweet blended song was always to be heard."

The immortal dwellers in this land could become invisible at will or even change their forms, e.g., to that of birds. The beauty of that world is described in the most ravishing terms, its cliffs, its plains, its hills, its waters, its summer haze, its lack of all that sometimes makes earth undesirable. Also there are its fertility and plenty: all growing things produced without toil.

There are tales, especially in Welsh tradition, of cattle stolen from the divine land, a form of the belief that the gifts of civilization were of divine origin, like the fire of Prometheus. Again a magic cauldron is spoken of, inexhaustible in its contents, capable of satisfying a multitude of people. Such a cauldron belonged to the god Dagda. The cauldron could restore life; it was also the source of inspiration. All these qualities made it desirable; hence there are stories of the theft of such a cauldron from the divine land.

This Wonderland must have been known to the Brythons, and it is called Annwfn in some tales, though this name, meaning the place of the dead or even hell in later times, has probably replaced an earlier pagan name. But where mentioned in surviving Welsh tales or poems, it is a Wonderland, on earth's surface, or beyond or under the sea. It is beautiful, its people are immortal, its cattle or other animals, its cauldron, are sometimes mentioned, and some of these were stolen. The name Avallon, a word probably connected with an earlier *aballos*, "apple," perhaps with reference to its marvellous apple-trees, like those in Irish tales, is applied to the Brythonic

Elysium in connexion with Arthur, who was taken there to be healed of his wounds. It is described in terms similar to those about the Irish divine land. Why it should have come to be identified with Glastonbury, as it was before the time of William of Malmesbury (twelfth century), is obscure.

The origin of this Celtic Wonderland belief cannot be stated with certainty. Did it originate from myths of a Golden Age, which are known to many races, when men dwelt nearer to the gods, and which they hoped to recover, or saw it in the immortal land and beautiful surroundings of the place of the deities? Or was it merely a romantic rendering of man's wishes that the troubles of earthly life might be overcome and an ideal world found or at least made the subject of dream? Whatever be the origin of these tales, they are impressive.

Here may be cited one which in many ways is characteristic of many of them, though in actual number as now existing they do not amount to more than a dozen. This tale is the *Echtra Condla*, Connla being the son of a king in the second century A.D. One day, invisible to all but him, appeared a beautiful woman who said that she came from Tir na mBeo, where was deathlessness. There, there was always feasting on food which needed no preparation. It was full of all that was desirable. She and the others dwelt in a great *síd* and were called *aes síd*, "people of the *síd*." Connla's father, Conn, asked him who spoke to him. She then said that for her there would be neither old age nor death. She loved his son and wished him to come to Mag Mell. Conn then commanded his Druid to act by magic upon her, so that she might neither be heard nor seen. She went away, after giving Connla an apple. This he ate: it never grew less, nor did he require other food. A month passed. She returned and called Connla to come, for the ever-living ones invited him. Again Conn bade his Druid to act. She said that the Druids would soon pass for ever (i.e., before the coming of St. Patrick—a Christian interpolation in the original story). The mysterious visitant said that once in her boat of glass Connla would forget the grief of parting. He leaped into the boat: it sped across the waves, and he was seen no more. In this tale the conception of the island Wonderland and that of the underground *síd* are confused.

In some of the tales it is shown to be dangerous for those invited to the immortal land to return to earth. This appears in the story of Bran and his companions. They were warned not to go back to earth or, if they did, not to set foot on it. One of his followers sprang to the shore when they returned, and became ashes. Bran had been gone for centuries, though to him and the others it had seemed but a year. Now he and the rest returned to the divine land.

This pagan Wonderland reappears in some later Christian documents regarding voyages of Christian saints, notably in the different versions of St. Brendan's voyages. He went to seek the Earthly Paradise, an island in the ocean, the Land of Promise of the Living Ones. The descriptions of it, its beauty, its peace, its wonders, are based on the old pagan tradition. That tradition of a world of lasting beauty and joy has never been surpassed. The tales describe what is found in the poetry and fancies of many peoples, but in a form unparalleled elsewhere, the human desire, but how exquisitely expressed, for a better, a more delectable, a more satisfying world than that of daily experience, a world

> "Where falls not hail, nor rain, nor any snow,
> Nor ever wind blows loudly; but it lies
> Deep-meadowed, happy, fair with orchard lawns,
> And bowery hollows crowned with summer seas",

a world which knew

> "Summers of the snakeless meadow, unlaborious earth
> and oarless sea".

CHAPTER XIV

MORALITY

IN moral standard the Celts were probably neither better nor worse than other barbaric peoples. The Gauls were monogamous. The wild statements made by Cæsar and others about ten or twelve men, brothers with brothers, fathers with sons, having wives in common, and by others about the Goidels in Ireland, who by their accounts seem to have lived in a state of free love and of incest, are impossible on the face of them, and have no support from the existing tales and other writings which have come down to us. No doubt there were those who committed adultery, and concubinage was permissible. But these things did not exceed the practices of most barbaric peoples.

Religious beliefs, especially those about the future life, made the Celts brave, casting from them the fear of death. Religious scruples prevented them from withholding spoil which should have been deposited in a sacred place, or from dishonestly taking what had been placed there. Did anyone transgress he was grievously punished, even with torture. Diodorus speaks of much gold deposited in temples and consecrated places as an offering for the gods. Out of religious scruples no one laid hands on this.

The anger of the gods fell on those who disobeyed them, though how far this was concerned with moral delinquency is not clear. But those who did not accept the judgment of the Druids on various matters were regarded as impious and debarred from the sacrifices, and this was a heavy penalty.

Irish tales hint that divine punishment followed breaches of divine law, though what that law was is not stated, but improper encroachment on sacred places was one of the things punished. In some tales the divine vengeance might fall on a descendant of the aggressor rather than upon himself. Others suggest that obedience to divinely appointed rules, e.g., tabus. was necessary to prevent serious calamities.

In one story of the Celtic Wonderland Manannan tells Bran that its people made love without crime. This seems to imply belief in a state where sexual relations were regulated, indeed a state where marriage was sacred. This appears in another tale in which the son of a sinless pair is required as a sacrifice for the sin of a goddess, Becuma, with a mortal king. Such a son had, as parents, the people of an Elysian land. His mother appeared and rescued him, giving an animal in his stead. The mortal king had lived in lawless love with Becuma for a year, and as a result there was famine in the land. This was in accordance with the view that a king should observe the *geasa*—things imposed upon him, and so preserve plenty in the land, or, as is implied, he was to be a good king. Here he had fallen from goodness, with evil results. Such ideas may not have been common. That they appear at all is striking.

The worst aspect of Celtic life was cruelty, especially where human sacrifice was concerned, and we have seen to what a degree this existed.

SCANDINAVIAN

CHAPTER I

SOURCES OF OUR KNOWLEDGE

THE Scandinavians were members of the Teutonic or Germanic peoples who, from central Europe, ultimately occupied Belgium, Switzerland, South Germany, penetrated into Italy—the Langobards or Lombards, and invaded England —the Angles and Saxons. Among the Scandinavians are included the Danes, Swedes, Norwegians, and the Icelanders who migrated to Iceland from Norway in the reign of Harold Haarfagr (the Fairhaired), ninth century, because of his oppression and on account of political troubles. The *Landnamabok* tells how, before they came to Iceland, men called *papas* had settled there, Christian monks from Ireland or Scotland. They did not remain after the coming of the pagan Norsemen, but elsewhere it is said that they left Irish books, bells and crosses behind them.

Opinions vary regarding the time when the respective lands were first entered by these Germanic tribes. The Danes may have occupied Denmark, when Angles and Saxons went to Britain, by the sixth century. At an earlier time Norway was occupied by tribes who drove before them the Finns and Lapps to the north. Perhaps earlier still Sweden was entered, two kindred peoples ultimately dwelling in the North and South.

From these countries came the bold and hardy sea-folk and warriors known as Northmen, who from the eighth century swarmed to England, the North and West of Scotland, Ireland and Normandy (the Normans), establishing themselves there, and who were long the terror of western Europe. They were also collectively known as the Vikings.

The conversion of these people to Christianity was not nearly complete until the eleventh century, and there were

many setbacks in the process, their faith in their own deities
and religious customs being deep-seated.

The religion of the Scandinavians was like that of the
Germanic tribes, and from our fuller knowledge of its Scandinavian form much of that of the Teutons has to be deduced.
It is certain that the chief deities and the religious practices
were the same over the whole Teutonic area.

For the Germanic tribes Cæsar is an early but somewhat
vague authority, asserting that they count as gods those only
whom they see or by whom they are openly aided—the Sun,
the Fire-god, and the Moon. He also says that they have no
Druids who regulate worship, and no interest in sacrifices—
the last statement being erroneous. He also speaks of the
custom of the German mothers declaring by lots and soothsaying the prospects of a fight. They said that it was against the
divine will if fighting began before the new moon.

Tacitus speaks from fuller knowledge in his account of
Germanic religion, but he seldom mentions the native names of
deities. In his chief account of the Germanic gods he says that
Mercury is the chief, propitiated with human victims; others
are Hercules and Mars. By these Roman deities are probably
meant Wodan, Donar or Thor, and Tyr. He says that the
Aestii worship the Mother of the gods, by whom Frigg may be
intended. One group of tribes, including the Naharvali,
worship Castor and Pollux; the Suevi performed sacred rites to
Isis, her symbol being a ship. What deities are intended by those
is not known. The native names of deities mentioned by Tacitus
are Nerthus, Tamfana, and Nehalennia; Tuisto, sprung from
the earth, was celebrated in the ancient songs, his son was
Mannus, whose three sons were progenitors of as many
tribes.

Here may be cited what Tacitus says of Nerthus, a goddess
worshipped by seven tribes of the Ingvæones on an island
identified with Seeland. They worship Nerthus or Mother
Earth, believing her to interpose in the affairs of men. On the
island is a very sacred grove in which is a chariot, held in great
reverence. It is covered with a veil, which the priest alone
may touch. At a certain time he is aware of her entrance into
the chariot. Cows are yoked to it and it is driven around the

country, great festivity being shown wherever the goddess comes. Everything was joyful at this season; there were no wars; arms were untouched. Everywhere is peace. The priest conducts the chariot back to the grove, and in a secret pool it and, if it may be believed, the goddess herself are washed. (Possibly the actual ceremony was that an image of the goddess was in the chariot.) Slaves perform this work and are swallowed up in the lake, a circumstance which causes great horror. The slaves were probably sacrificed. Further reference will be made to Nerthus when we come to consider the god Njord.

Besides the Roman writers there are notices in lives of saints and other ecclesiastical writings, and the evidence of folk-lore and folk-tradition.

For the most part we are dependent upon Scandinavian sources, which are fairly abundant, and which not only give a good view of Scandinavian religion, but may be suggestive for that of the Teutons generally.

First of all, come the Eddas, poetic and prose. The Poetic Edda contains in the first part poems about the gods, in the second part poems about heroic personages. The first part gives much information about the nature of the deities, the myths told about them, the beliefs in the future life and cosmogony, especially that strange and moving story of the Doom of the gods. For the last we are mainly indebted to the poem *Voluspa*, where the god Odin consults a *volva* or wise-woman, here regarded as more or less supernatural, about the future. Much information is contained also in *Váfthruthnismal*, a dialogue between Odin and the wise giant Vafthruthnir, and in *Grimnismal*, in which Odin, as Grimnir, tells much about the gods, their dwellings, and other matters. Other poems in the first part are of varying interest, but give many suggestive hints about the religious beliefs and customs of Scandinavia.

Of the heroic poems, while some are of German origin, all alike give many notices of the heroic ideals as well as glimpses of beliefs, e.g., of that in the Valkyries.

These poems were composed from the tenth century onwards, and thus in the pagan period. Christian influences have been seen in some of them, but if these actually exist, they are slight and of no great importance.

The Prose Edda is of later date and was composed by Snorri Sturluson, twelfth-thirteenth century. He was the son of an Icelandic chief, himself a chief, and a Christian. Yet in his book, especially in the first section of it—*Gylfaginning*, in which Gylfi, a Swedish King, went to Asgard, the home of the gods, was entertained there and heard much about the deities and their doings, there is a recital of numerous myths about the gods. It is strange that one who was a Christian should have thus collected and arranged this account of the pagan deities, myths, and legends of the past, with constant quotations from stanzas of the Poetic Edda. But he had a strong antiquarian interest in the vanished past and desired to give as complete an account of it as was possible. And he wished to give subjects to the skalds or poets, especially to those who were beginners in the art, he himself being a skald of no mean order.

Following *Gylfaginning* there is a long section called *Skaldskaparmal*, or the language of poetry, beginning with an account given by Bragi, the god of poetry, of the stealing of the goddess Idunn and the apples of immortality by the giant Thjazi, and of the manner in which Odin acquired the mead of poetry. This is followed by the rules which tell how gods, men, and things are to be described in metaphors, with numerous examples taken from the poets. A special language was used by poets, the *kenningar*, or kennings, metaphors to describe the subjects treated of. Thus there are numerous kennings to describe Odin, Thor, etc., man, woman, battle, weapons, armour, and many other things.

The third part, *Hattatal*, gives two of Snorri's own verse compositions.

Snorri warns the youthful skald not to tamper with the old kennings which chief skalds had used, and, again, as Christians, not to believe in the old gods nor in the truth of the tales set forth. Hence the Prologue to his Edda begins with an account of Creation, the Flood, and how men fell away from God. Then he relates how the gods were men, derived from Troy, and how Odin and his sons wandered thence to Scandinavia. This rationalizing of the gods is not followed in the main part of the book, but it is elaborated in another work of Snorri's, the *Ynglinga Saga*, the opening part of his *Heimskringla* or stories of the Kings of Norway.

The works called Sagas belong to the period of great literary activity in Iceland, beginning in the early part of the twelfth century, but some of their contents are based on the oral traditions of the old Saga reciters. In the main historical and biographical, the Sagas contain much that is fictitious. They tell of the Icelandic settlers and families, of the Norwegian Kings, and other personages. They are full of adventure, sea-faring, fighting, and the like. For the pagan religion of Scandinavia, especially of Iceland and Norway, they give much information which supplements what is known from other sources. Of special importance for this are the *Njal's Saga*, the *Eyrbyggia Saga*, *Egil's Saga*, *Vigaglum's Saga*, which form part of the collection known as *Islendinga Sögur*; the *Hervarar Saga*, and *Gautrek's Saga*, contained in the *Fornaldar Sögur*; the *Grettis Saga*, and Snorri's *Heimskringla*, already mentioned.

Another work of some importance is the *Gesta Danorum* of Saxo Grammaticus, himself a Dane, whose period is the twelfth century. Here are glimpses of myths and religious practices, though such deities as appear are regarded more or less as mortals. Saxo made use of earlier material, written or traditional. Adam of Bremen's work dealing with the history of the archbishops of Bremen has some useful information regarding the religious practices of the Swedes. He died in 1075, and thus lived sufficiently near to the pagan period for reliance to be placed on his statements.

CHAPTER II

MYTHICAL CONCEPTIONS

T H E myths of the Scandinavian peoples regarding their deities are much more copious than the accounts of their religion. That these myths in all their fullness were known to the people generally is more than doubtful. They were, if not invented, at least elaborated by the skalds and perhaps recited by them at gatherings of the chiefs and their retainers. We depend for our knowledge of the religion, of the nature of the gods, and of the worship paid to them, partly on those myths, partly on scattered notices in the literature, earlier or later.

Two groups of deities are distinguished, e.g., in the Prose Edda, the Æsir and the Vanir. The singular form of Æsir is Áss, and this word, if it is right to regard it as connected etymologically with Sanskrit *anas*, "breath" or "wind," would suggest that the gods were at first spirits. Later, however, the word meant "god." The Æsir were the gods. The Vanir include Njord, Frey, and Freyja, and possibly others. In the later stages these were included among the Æsir. They are more distinctly nature deities than these, producing fertility, though also having wider functions. Now there are differing myths which tell of war between the Æsir and the Vanir, and of the hostages which they gave to each other.

This war is first alluded to in *Voluspa*, in which it is called the first war in the world. The gods smote Gollveig with spears, and burned her thrice. Thrice she came alive. She was Heidh, a being skilled in magic. Odin hurled his spear over the Vanir, devoting them to destruction, but they were victorious, and broke down the wall of the gods' citadel. Then the gods debated whether to pay tribute or to admit the Vanir to equal worship. In the Prose Edda Snorri tells how the Vanir gave Njord as hostage to the gods, while these gave them Hœnir. This is elaborated in the *Ynglinga Saga* which puts this war at the time when Odin and others were by Snorri rationalized as men—chiefs and kings. Both Vanir and Odin's

100

folk harried each other's lands, now one, now the other, prevailing. Then came a truce, peace was made, and each side gave hostages to the other. The Vanir gave Njord and Frey; Odin's people gave Hœnir and Mimir, wisest of men. But at all assemblies, at the discussion of any hard matter, Hœnir would never give an opinion unless Mimir was beside him. The Vanir were suspicious and resentful and, cutting off Mimir's head, sent it to Odin, who took means to preserve it, sang charms over it, and consulted it when there was need.

This war is not, as in myths of other races, one between deities of light and growth on the one hand, and of darkness and blight on the other. It is easiest to regard it as the mythical reflection of an opposition between worshippers of certain deities in one region, and those, possibly incomers, who worshipped another group. This is best explained by the existence of the Vanir worship at an early time in Sweden and Norway, followed by the introduction of the worship of Odin from some part of Germany. The strife of rival forms of worship might continue for some time until a compromise was effected, and both groups of deities accepted by all. At all events the Vanir are given place along with the Æsir. Though goddesses are included in these groups, they are spoken of also as a separate group, the Asynjur, not less holy nor of less authority than the gods. Frigg, Odin's consort, is chief of these, but most of the others are little more than names.

In the *Ynglinga Saga*, Snorri elaborates what he had said in his Prologue to the Prose Edda about Odin and others being kings and coming from the East. He makes them human and yet they are more than human. Asgard was a city, its chief Odin, east of Tanais which flows into the Black Sea. Odin was a great warrior and conqueror and a great traveller. Once when he was away for a long time his brothers Vili and Ve ruled for him. The people thought he had gone for ever, so the brothers shared his property and both took his consort Frigg to wife. Odin now came home. Then follows the account of the Vanir war, and how Odin made Njord and Frey temple-priests, with Freyja, skilled in magic, as temple-priestess. Njord had married his sister, according to Vanir custom; their children were Frey and Freyja. Odin now fared into other

lands and came to Sweden and made a great temple with blood
sacrifices, and gave good dwelling-places to Njord, Frey,
Heimdall, Thor, and Balder.

Odin knew many crafts. He was much honoured, especially
for the terror caused by his face in war, but also for his power
of shape-shifting, and his great gift in skald-craft. In war he
could make his foes blind, deaf, or terror-stricken. Much is
said about his magic, his power over nature, his consulting
with Mimir's head. He taught by means of runes and spells.
He could tell the future and how to work ill to whom he desired.
All these things he taught to the temple-priests, and so much
were he and they honoured that men paid them sacrifice and
called them gods. Then Odin died, and was marked with a
spear-point. He claimed as his own all who should die by
weapons. He would now go to the land whence he had come
and would welcome his friends there. So, as he would live for
ever, now his worship and vowing of vows to him increased.

Njord now became ruler and there were great peace and
plenty in his time, so much so that it was thought he ruled
abundance and wealth. Then he died and Frey succeeded him.
These also were good years when he ruled. He built and
endowed his temple at Uppsala. The "Peace of Frodi" and
years of plenty prevailed in his time, and all this was ascribed
to him and he was much loved. Gerd was his wife: Fjolnir
their son. Then Frey fell sick and died, and was not cremated
but buried in a great howe and it was given out that he was
still alive. Years of plenty and peace still prevailed.

Freyja alone of the deities now remained and she was held
in great fame. All the Swedes now knew that Frey was dead.
The good and plentiful years still prevailed, and it was thought
that these would continue as long as he remained in Sweden.
Hence his body was kept in the howe. He was called god of the
world, and sacrifice to him continued, especially for plenty
and peace.

In these chapters of the *Ynglinga Saga*, the author seems
to sway between his desire to make the chief gods into Kings
and an impulse to prove their more than human powers,
according to the beliefs, traditions, and myths of his pagan
ancestors. It is curious, however, that nothing is said of the fate

of Thor, Heimdall, and Balder, spoken of earlier in this curious account.

The gods dwell in Asgard, a district, or a citadel, either in heaven, or raised above the earth's surface, but most have a separate dwelling or hall, each for himself or herself. How far or in what regions all the deities enumerated by Snorri in the Prose Edda were worshipped cannot be definitely known.

Some may have been local deities, like many found among the Celts, though there is no evidence that the Scandinavians possessed so many of these as the Celts in Gaul. The lesser deities, apart from those who, like Thor, Odin, Frey, had a widespread worship, may have been little more than inventions of the skalds.

The Scandinavian deities are not immortal. Like those of the Irish Celts the renewal of youth or their continued existence depends on their eating the apples of Idunn when they begin to feel old, as they did when the giant Thyaji stole these apples. Yet in descriptions of the gods they show no sign of feebleness, but myth told of the Doom awaiting them, and Balder, young and beautiful, was slain and was lamented by the gods.

As in most religions and mythologies there is a certain dualism to be observed in Scandinavian religion, the opposition of monstrous, more or less evil beings to deities. This is seen in the hostility of giants, whose abode is Jötunheim, to the Æsir. Yet this opposition can hardly be called a moral dualism. The gods are not described as highly ethical, nor are giants and monsters necessarily immoral.

The Romans, especially Tacitus, equated some of the gods of the Germanic tribes with their own deities, as has been seen.

Some Christian writers made similar identifications. Adam of Bremen, c. 1075, speaking of three images of Thor, Odin, and Frey, in the temple at Uppsala, notes their respective likeness to Jupiter, Mars, and Priapus. Earlier than he, Ælfric regards Thor as Jupiter, Odin as Mercury, Frigg as Venus. These identifications, like those of the Romano-Gaulish ones, can at best be but partial.

In spite of the many myths or stories about the gods both in the Poetic and Prose Eddas, and elsewhere, it is difficult, save occasionally, to extract from these clear indications of the functions of these deities or of how they stood in relation to their worshippers.

Snorri's account of the gods makes Odin the chief god, the All-father, their head, the others being his family or grouped around him as his court. This is possibly not his own invention, but continued by him as a tradition handed down by skalds and court poets from the time when Odin's worship had been organized and made prominent in the courtly circles. It was then necessary to bring the other deities into relationship with him, even when they had been worshipped before his appearance among the Scandinavians. Some of the poems in the Poetic Edda have glimpses of the same grouping as appears in the Prose Edda. Odin may not have been a deity native to the Scandinavians, though his incoming and his acceptance by aristocratic circles, as well as his position as a war-god in an increasingly warlike era, gave him a prominence over such gods as Thor and Frey.

CHAPTER III

SCANDINAVIAN DEITIES

A CHRISTIAN writer, Paul the Deacon, speaks of Wodan as a god worshipped by all the German people. The name of this chief deity varies, Wuotan in Old High German, Saxon Wodan, Norse Odin. Whatever his origin he had risen to be the chief god of many of the Teutonic peoples, and his various functions, whether as a god of the sky, of war, of the winds, of the dead, of poetry and poetic inspiration, are found more or less wherever he was known and worshipped. Snorri, as a later mythographer, and concerning himself only with things as he, a skald, viewed them, assigns to Odin a supreme position. He is ruler of heaven and earth, highest of the Æsir, whom the other gods, his children, mighty as they are, serve as children obey a father. Hence he is called All-father. Another name of his is Val-father, "father of the slain," because those who fall in battle are chosen by him, collected by the Valkyries, and received into Valhall. He arranges wars and battles, and gives power to men against their enemies. This aspect of Odin as god of war is supported by Adam of Bremen. Odin, that is *Furor*, attends to wars, gives men strength against enemies. Adam identifies him with Mars, and says that his image is armed like that of Mars. Human sacrifices were made to him as god of war, before or during or after a battle. They were given to him in hope of victory or as a thanksgiving for it.

In heaven is Valaskjalf, possessed by Odin, thatched with silver, with its hall Hlidskjalf, whence Odin can survey all lands, looking from his window, as Paul the Deacon explains. At his table Odin gives the food set for him to his wolves, Geri and Freki. He needs no food, wine sufficing him for food and drink. Two ravens sit on his shoulders and speak into his ear all things seen and heard by them, for at sunrise he sends them forth over the world to collect tidings. His steed Sleipnir, best and swiftest of steeds, had eight feet and carried him through the air. His spear, Gungnir, was made by dwarfs and never missed in its thrust. According to *Voluspa* its hurling over the Vanir caused the first war in the world. The Vanir had been consecrated thus to destruction, and such a casting of a spear over a hostile force, devoting it to Odin along with an appeal to the god for victory, was common.

As a result of his supremacy Odin was recognized as father of the other deities. His name also occurs in genealogies, e.g., those of the Anglo-Saxon kings, who are traced back to him, the god himself being regarded as first of the kingly line.

The *Hyndluljoth* speaks of his gifts to men or to special men, to Hermod a coat of mail and helmet, to Sigmund a sword, to others gold, armour, arms, triumph, treasure, his art to the singer, fair winds to sailors, wisdom and skill in words to others. His wisdom is emphasized in the *Vafthruthnismal* and elsewhere, and he was particularly regarded as god of poetry and bardic eloquence. In *Havamal* he is called "King of Singers," and the *Ynglinga Saga* tells how he taught skald-craft, the art of poetry, as well as runes and magic songs. On his favourite Starkad he bestowed the gift of verse. One myth tells how he became possessor of the mead of poetry, which he gives to poets. Poetry is Odin's drink, or gift, or booty. To obtain this mead he had to change his shape, and shape-shifting, no less than all kinds of magic, were often ascribed to him.

Odin was lord of life and death, and human sacrifices were offered to him by those who wished their lives to be prolonged. Indeed, it was mainly to him that human victims were offered.

There are few references to Odin's supremacy in Iceland and Norway, where Thor was pre-eminent. Probably he was more important in Denmark and Sweden, if his worship reached these lands from Germany. Yet even in Sweden, his image had not the central place. Thor's image had that of Odin on one side and of Fricco (Frey) on the other. Possibly Odin's supremacy was due to his being the god of the aristocracy, or to the court poets in the Viking age helping to give him a higher place. Odin's position is not unlike that of a king in his court. Though the words are not supported elsewhere, in the *Harbardsljoth*, a burlesque flyting between Thor and Odin as Harbard, the latter says that Odin has the nobles who fall in battle, while Thor has the peasants. Thor is here represented as more or less uncouth. He may have retained the affection of the people when the higher classes were giving more allegiance to Odin.

Vili and Ve, described as Odin's brothers by Snorri, all three being sons of the giant Bor, and together taking part in creation (p. 155), are otherwise unknown, except that in the *Ynglinga Saga* they are set over his realm when Odin journeys. Once when he was a long time away and it was thought that he would not return they took his consort Frigg in marriage between them. Frigg is scornfully attacked for this by Loki in the *Lokasenna*.

The god called Donar in Germany, Thunor by the Saxons, was in Scandinavia Thor, the name meaning the Thunderer. He is represented in all the vigour of life, with a red beard. When he blows into this the thunder is heard. But his functions were much more numerous than that of a thunder-god. His symbol was his hammer, Mjollnir, forged by dwarfs, and known to the giants, among whose race it had done much ill. This hammer was primarily the lightning-bolt. Thor was strongest of the gods, and his strength was increased when his "girdle of might" was clasped about him. To wield his hammer he put on iron gloves. He is never depicted as riding, but walking or driving in his wagon, drawn by he-goats. The rolling of the wagon represents the rolling of thunder. As thunder-god he is the equivalent of Jupiter, and this equation is frequently found, but he was also equated with Hercules for his strength. Thor's hall, Bilskirnir, is in Thrudvangar, "the plains of strength."

Besides being a thunder-god, Thor was also a god of fertility, since the showers, especially those which accompanied thunder, produced a fuller growth. This is spoken of by Adam of Bremen. "Thor rules thunder and lightning, winds and showers, and the fair fruits of the earth." This may be connected with the fact that Jörd, Earth, is his mother. That Odin was said to be his father may be regarded as due to the growing pre-eminence of Odin, and to the skalds. Thor was still the chief god in Norway as well as among the settlers in Iceland, some of whom called upon him as their beloved friend and sought his guidance about the place of their settlement in Iceland. There were many temples to Thor in Norway, Sweden, and Iceland, and there are very many personal and place-names compounded with Thor. In the records of the settlers in Iceland it is often told how, before reaching the coast, they cast overboard their high-seat pillars on which an image of Thor was carved, and, where these drifted ashore, no matter how long this took or in whatsoever place, they made their final settlement. The belief was that Thor would cause these to drift where he wished their owners to settle, a vow being sometimes made to him for that purpose. That site was then dedicated to Thor, and a temple built to him.

In the many myths about Thor he is represented as warring against giants, monsters, trolls, and dwarfs.

Thursday is named from him, and this day had special observances which were condemned in early medieval ecclesiastical documents. On the whole Thor was a beneficent god to his worshippers. Sacrifices to him were mainly of animals and foodstuffs, though the Norman Vikings offered him human victims, before setting out on their raids.

A god whose worship was widespread among the Teutons was Zio (in Old High German), Tyw (in Anglo-Saxon), or Tyr (in Scandinavia). Zio was equated with Mars by later writers, and he is the Mars of whom Tacitus speaks. He was thus a great war-god, and he evidently occupied a high place among the Teutons. To him human sacrifices were offered. The name of the third day of the week, Tuesday, is taken from his name and is of wide occurrence—O.H.G. Ziestag, A.S. Tiwesdaeg, Swedish Tisdag, Danish Tirsdag, Norse Tyrsdagr. In baptismal renunciation of heathenism among the Saxons Thunar, Woden, and Saxnot or Sahsnot (Swordbearer) who seems to stand for Mars or Tyr are specially included as objects of renunciation. Of Tyr Snorri says that he is most daring and stout of heart, and has much power over victory in battle. It is good for brave men to worship him. He is called "god of battles." He then cites epithets applied to men, "Tyrvaliant," one who exceeds in valour, "Tyrprudent," one who is wise. The *Sigrdrifumal*, speaking of runes for victory, adds "call twice on Tyr." At one time Tyr may have occupied as high a place as Odin, if not higher, but with the growing position of that god, he seems to fade out of actual worship, and becomes

Odin's son. Myth explains why he is one-handed, as deities elsewhere are sometimes said to be. The gods learned that the monstrous brood of Loki would cause them misfortune. Of these they brought home the Fenris-wolf, then of small size. Tyr alone dared to feed him, but as he grew in size daily, it was resolved to chain him. But he broke every fetter, and another, Gleipnir, was made by dwarfs. The wolf scorned it, but bargained that one of the gods should put his hand in the wolf's mouth while he was being bound with it. None was willing, till Tyr volunteered. This fetter was magically made, it bound the wolf, and in his struggle, Tyr's hand was bitten off by him. Loki taunts Tyr with this in the *Lokasenna*. The *Hymiskvitha* calls the giant Hymir father of Tyr, and Tyr and Thor go to obtain his kettle. At the Doom of the gods Tyr fights with the watch-dog of Hel, Garm, and each slays the other.

Balder, whose name means "bright" or "shining," and from whom light shines, was son of Odin and Frigg. He was wisest of the gods, gracious and kindly of speech. His judgments were not to be gainsaid. He mainly appears as the subject of myths. One of these tells how he had evil dreams and how the gods sought means for his safety. Frigg took oaths of all things, the mistletoe excepted, that they should not hurt him. Now it became a diversion of the gods to make him the object of blows or missiles, with certainty that nothing would hurt him. Loki, by cunning, learned that Frigg had taken no oath of the mistletoe, because it was too young. The blind god, Hödr, took no part in the sport of the Æsir, but Loki gave him mistletoe and said that he would direct his hand. This was done and Balder fell dead. Nanna, his consort, died of grief, and both were burned in his ship on a huge pyre. Hermodr rode to Hel to ransom Balder, who had gone thither. Hel said that he could return if all wept for him. When the gods heard this they sent everywhere to get all to mourn. But the giantess Thokk, Loki in disguise, refused. Balder thus remained in Hel. This is Snorri's account, but some of the Eddic poems seem to lay the blame on Hödr alone, and tell how Odin now begat a son Vali by a giantess, and he, when he was a day old, slew Hödr. This is supported by the long story in Saxo Grammaticus in which

Hotherus (Hödr) slays Balder with a magic sword. Interpretations of the Balder myth have been many, but none are satisfactory.

Hödr, the blind god, so imagined, according to Grimm, because he dealt out good or ill fortune at random, was known as "Balder's bane." Snorri described him as very strong, but adds that the gods desire him not to be named, for his work will long remain in memory. Possibly in an older myth there may have been enmity between the brothers, Balder and Hödr, and Balder in one kenning is called "adversary of Hödr." After the Doom of the gods, both return from Hel and, now reconciled, share in the new world of peace. Vali is also with them.

Of a cult of Heimdall, "the white god," son of Odin, nothing is known. He is the watchman of the gods, sitting on the verge of their land to guard it from the giants. He needs less sleep than a bird, sees as well by night as by day, and hears the grass grow. He is said to be the son of nine giant women, possibly the nine who are the waves personified, and made strong with the strength of earth, sea, and sacrificial blood. His horn, the Gjallar-horn, is heard through all worlds, and will awake the gods before their doom.

Bragi was the god of skaldic eloquence (*bragr*, "poetry"), the first maker of poetry, and probably worshipped by skalds. His consort was Idunn.

Ullr was son of Thor's wife Sif. His abode is Ydalir, "yewdale," appropriate to one who was the divine archer. He is described as fair of aspect, and swiftest of all on snow-shoes, besides being famed as a warrior. Snorri says that it is good to call on him in single combat. He is called god of the bow and god of the snow-shoe.

Forseti, son of Balder, had a heavenly abode, Glitnir, with golden pillars and roofed with silver. It was regarded as a seat of judgment, and those who, having legal quarrels, approached him, were reconciled. Thus he was a god of judgment to whom appeal was made by suitors. Among the Frisians a god Fosite, who is assumed to be Forseti, had a highly sacred place on Heligoland or Fosite's land. Here were his temples, and the place was so venerated that none dared touch the animals grazing there. Water might be drawn from the spring only in silence. Violators of these rules were put to death by order of the king. St. Willibrord baptized men in the spring and ordered some of the cattle to be slain for food. The islanders thought he was mad or would perish. But the king cast lots about putting him to death. These were favourable to the saint.

Hœnir is named with Odin and Loki (here called Lothur, and without evil traits), in two incidents. First, when they are travelling, they find two trees which they make into a human pair, Lothur giving them heat. Second, they capture the dwarf Andvari and take his gold. We have seen how he was given as a hostage to the Vanír. Hœnir survives the Doom of the gods and has the prophetic wand or can foretell things to come. Nothing is known of his divine functions nor whether worship was paid to him.

Vidarr, "the silent god," son of Odin, had strength nearly as great as Thor's, and the gods placed confidence in him in all struggles. His land Vithi is full of trees and tall grass, which may suggest that he was a god of the woods. At the Doom of the gods he slew the Fenris wolf, and survived into the new world.

Ægir, a giant god of the sea (ægir, "sea"), is not one of the Æsir though more or less on friendly terms with them. He entertained the gods, who had found through divination that he had much provision for a feast. Odin bade him prepare for them, and now he asked them to bring a suitable kettle. This was done to cause trouble to the gods for their imposing on him for entertainment. The kettle was hard to obtain, but at last it was procured and the feast began. At the feast Loki slew one of Ægir's servants. Light in Ægir's hall was provided by gold (hence gold was called "water's flame" or "fire of the sea"). Snorri represents Ægir as being feasted by the gods, when Bragi told him tales about them and about the origin of the mead of poesy, and how the skalds used metaphors for all things. The island of Hlesey, Lösö in the Kattegat, was Ægir's island, another name of his being Hler. He represents the sea in its milder aspect.

Loki, a personage mainly of myths, though included among the Æsir, was son of a giant. He joins in adventures with the gods, as with Hœnir and Odin, but mostly he is a personification of malicious mischief. He is said to bring the gods into great hardships, and again, by his craft, to relieve them. He is brought into the mythology to explain certain beings and doings. Thus he is father of the monsters, the Fenris wolf and Midgard serpent, and of Hel, by the giantess Angrboda. He causes Balder's death. He is an expert at changing his shape. Possibly Loki was an earlier elemental deity, a fire-god, since as Lothur he gives heat to the first created human pair, but nothing can be definitely said of a being with so many aspects.

A somewhat enigmatic being is Mimir. Snorri describes his well as being under one of the roots of the ash Yggdrasil; in it wisdom and understanding are stored. Mimir is wise and knows old things. He drinks of the well, using the Gjallar-horn. Odin came and begged a draught from the well, but had to give his eye as a pledge to Mimir. Now it is hidden in the well, as *Voluspa* says, and Mimir uses it to water the tree and to drink mead. Thus it has become a vessel. Snorri quotes a poem in which Mimir is called the friend of Odin.

Another version of the Mimir story is given in the *Ynglinga Saga*. Mimir, wisest of men, was given as a hostage to the Vanir, who cut off his head and sent it to the Æsir. Odin preserved it and sang charms over it, so that it spoke to him of hidden matters. *Sigrdrifumal* tells how Odin learned runes from the head. *Voluspa*, contradictory to what it had said of Mimir himself, goes on to tell how at the Doom of the gods Odin goes to consult, not him, as a living being, but his head. Snorri also speaks of Odin seeking advice of Mimir at the Doom, but not of the head. Mimir is supremely wise. He is perhaps Mimingus, a satyr of the woods in Saxo's version of the Balder story. In the *Vilkina Saga* Mimir is a smith by whom Velint is instructed. Mimir, guardian of a most sacred well, may have been the spirit of the waters or a semi-divine being connected with these. The belief in a head with wisdom or power has been met with in Celtic story.

Njörd, one of the Vanir but later joined with the Æsir, "the sinless ruler of men," dwells in Noatun, "ship-haven," in heaven. He rules the course of the wind and stills sea and fire. Men appeal to him for voyages and hunting. Himself wealthy he bestows wealth on men. One poem speaks of his numerous temples. His consort was Skadi, daughter of the giant Thyaji, dwelling at Thrymheim in the mountains. Skadi would fain have dwelt there still, but Njörd wished to be near the sea. They made a compact to live nine nights at Thrymheim and nine at Noatun. But neither was satisfied. Njörd is a god worshipped by sea-farers, those first who dwelt on the coasts of the Baltic whence the cult spread to Norway, where his name occurs in place-names, as well as one who gives prosperity to these.

The connexion between Njörd and the goddess Nerthus of the Ingvaeones (see p. 96) has been much discussed. The names are alike. Was Tacitus mistaken in speaking of a goddess? Or was Njörd a consort of Nerthus? Were they brother and sister, as Snorri speaks of Njörd marrying a sister? These and other theories have been upheld. Njörd, as a god of wealth, may have had to do with fertility, like Nerthus and like his son Frey. This group of Vanir deities, Njörd, with Nerthus, Frey, and Freyja, might be native deities of the Swedes, before the worship of Odin was brought among them. Frey is sometimes called Yngvi-Frey, as by Snorri (in *Lokasenna* Ingunar-Frey), as if he were connected with the Ingvaeones, and also he is described as Sviagodh or god of the Swedes.

Njörd had a high place in Scandinavian worship along with the better known Frey, his name being coupled at toasts with his.

Frey and Freyja were Njörd's son and daughter. Frey had a high place among the gods, for he is called the most famous of the Æsir and is described as ruling over rain and sunshine and the fruit of the earth. Men called on him for fruitful seasons and peace. His seat was in Alfheim. His special possessions were the magic ship Skidbladnir and the boar Gullinbursti or Goldbristles. His worship was popular in Sweden and Norway and its chief seat was at Uppsala where the temple was said to have been raised by himself and endowed with all his wealth. This is from the *Ynglinga Saga*, which regards the gods first as kings. He was called lord of the Swedes and god of the Swedes, and peace and plenty were abundant in his time. To him sacrifices were made for years of abundance and for peace.

His image in this temple by its attributes plainly showed that he was a god of fertility. Thence his image was drawn on a wagon at the end of winter through the land, accompanied by his priestess, regarded as his wife, and in one story an impostor took the place of the image and demanded gold, silver, and raiment instead of the ordinary sacrifices. From Sweden Frey's cult passed to Norway and Iceland, where several notices in the Sagas show his importance. Hrafnkel built a large temple for him, loving no god so much as Frey and giving him half of his goods, and he was known as Frey's *godi* or priest. In *Vigaglum's Saga* Thorkel was anxious that Glum should be driven off the land, and he sacrificed an old steer to Frey, who had received many gifts from him, and begging his help in this. The steer fell dead, and Thorkel esteemed this a good omen. Long after, Glum dreamt that he saw many people coming to visit Frey who sat on a chair. He learned that these were his kindred begging Frey that he should not be driven out, but Frey answered angrily, recalling the sacrifice of Thorkel's. We hear also of silver amulets of Frey by which another settler was led to the site of his house in Iceland. There are many references to Frey's priests. At Throndhjeim he had a temple, in which prayer was made to him for fertility. The procession of his image with its priestess guardian through the land from Uppsala is exactly parallel with that of Nerthus, and is a farther evidence of the connexion of the Vanir group with her. At the drinking of toasts at festivals, while that of Odin was drunk for victory, there were two others, to Njörd and to Frey for plenty and for peace.

The goddesses are collectively known as the Asynjur, and Snorri includes among these Frigg, Freyja, Gefjun, Idunn, Gerd, Eir, Sigyn, Fulla, Saga, Sjofn, Lofn, Vár, Vör, Syn, Snotra, Gna, Sol, Bil, Hlin, Jörd, Rind. Some of these are named merely as consorts of gods, some as attendants upon the greater goddesses, and of most of them little is known.

Of these the greatest is Frigg, no doubt because of Odin's later pre-eminence. She was known to the Teutonic tribes as Frija, as in the Merseberg charm which mentions her, and among the Lombards as Frea. She gave her name to the sixth day of the week, in Old High German, Anglo-Saxon, Frisian and Norse, which shows that she was widely known and worshipped. She is consort of Odin, and thus mother of the Æsir in Snorri's reckoning. She is said to be foremost of the Asynjur. She was goddess of marriage and giver of children, and was invoked by the childless. She is said to know the fates of men, but to keep silence about this. Her own abode is Fensalir, "sea-halls," a glorious dwelling, but she shares with Odin his abode of Hlithskjolf. By her unwittingly Balder was slain, for she omitted the mistletoe when she took oaths of all things not to hurt him, though she wept much for Valhall's need at his death. Odin took counsel with her, e.g., about his visit to the wise giant Vafthruthnir to find out his wisdom.

Freyja, one of the Vanir, and daughter of Njörd, was renowned and beautiful. Her heavenly mansion was called Folkvangr, "Field of the folk" ; her hall Sessrumnir, "rich in seats," large and fair. She was goddess of love, and it was appropriate to call upon her for success in love. Love-songs were liked by her, and she answered men's prayers. The *Hyndluljoth* speaks of her altar of stone, which had become fused like glass because of the fires kindled on it and reddened with the blood of sacrifices. Along with Odin she has half of the slain, and she might thus be regarded as chief of the Valkyries, but here as elsewhere she may have been confused with Frigg. She has a feather-dress, used in flying, and she drives in a car drawn by cats. She was sought by giants, by the giant artificer, who rebuilt the gods' abode, and by Thrym. Her consort was Odr, to whom she was devoted. When he went on long journeys, she wept and her tears were tears of gold, and she went seeking him, calling herself by different names. Their daughter is the beautiful Hnoss. In the *Oddrunargratr* she is coupled with Frigg as ministering healing. Freyja may be the Vanir woman whom the gods ill-treated, and who is called in *Voluspa* Gollveig, "might of gold," and Heidr, a woman full of magic, just as Freyja was first to teach it among the Æsir, according to the *Ynglinga Saga*.

Idunn guarded in her chest the apples of immortality which renewed the youth of the gods when they grew old. An idea such as this is found in other mythologies, e.g., Celtic (p. 89), for gods are not necessarily immortal. The giant

Thjazi, who had Loki in his power, forced him to bring Idunn and the apples to a wood, where he, as an eagle, flew with them to Thrymheim. Then the gods, troubled at this, became old, and caused Loki to recover Idunn and the apples. Idunn was consort of Bragi, god of poetry.

Gefjun had sons born to a giant, an example of the occasional commingling of deities and giants. On the other hand Snorri speaks of her as a virgin, and that they who die maidens attend her. In the opening paragraph of *Gylfaginning* a wandering woman entertains Gylfi, King of Sweden, who gives her as a reward a ploughland in his kingdom. The woman was Gefjun and she brought her four sons by the giant and yoked them to a plough. According to the *Ynglinga Saga* she first transformed them to oxen. The result was that much of the land was removed to sea and formed Seelund. Water took the place of the land where the removed land had been. In *Lokasenna*, when Gefjun is defamed by Loki, Odin speaks out and says that she knows the fate set for all, even as he himself does, just as, later in this poem, Frigg is said to have the same knowledge. Hence it has been held that Gefjun is a form of Frigg, perhaps a localized form of Odin's consort. The *Ynglinga Saga* says that Odin's son Skjold married Gefjun. Skjold was god of the Skanians, the Danish people of the island of Skaane, and the supposed ancestor of the kings of Denmark, the Skjoldings. Thus Gefjun's worship may have been Danish, but nothing is known of this. Whether she was identical with Freyja, as has been claimed, or whether the goddess Gefjun and the Gefjun of the island myth are separate personages, is uncertain. The formation of the island is a minor creation myth.

Gerd, included among the Asynjur, was the beautiful daughter of the hill-giant Gymir. Frey had occupied Odin's place in Hlidskjolf and, looking over the world, saw Gerd, from whose person brightness gleamed over all. His pride in occupying Odin's seat had a fall, for after seeing Gerd, he was full of sorrow, and could neither sleep, eat, or drink. Njörd sent Skirnir, Frey's servant, to enquire what had befallen him. This he learned, and was sent by Frey to woo her on his behalf. Skirnir went on Frey's horse which would ride through fire, for Gymir's house was surrounded by flames, and armed at his request, with Frey's sword which fought of itself. Gerd refused to meet with Frey, though Skirnir threatened her with the direst ills if she would not. At last she agreed, and said that she would meet Frey nine nights hence at a certain forest. Thus she became his consort. Snorri tells this tale, and it is the subject of the poem *Skirnismal*, one of the finest in the Edda. It is notable because in it Frey complains that none of the Æsir, none of the Alfar, will help him to gain his desire. Gerd also asks Skirnir if he is of the Æsir, Vanir, or Alfar. Nothing further is known of Gerd. Apparently Skirnir kept Frey's sword, for he failed to have it at the Doom of the gods, when Surtr slew him because he lacked it.

Little is known of Fulla who is called Frigg's servant. Snorri speaks of her as a maid, with loose tresses and a golden band round her head. Hence gold was called Fulla's fillet. She bore a coffer belonging to Frigg, had charge of her sandals, and knew her secret counsel. In the tenth century Merseburg manuscript there is a charm for the healing of a colt, which tells how, when Balder's colt was lamed, both Fruwa and Volla, her sister, charmed the lamed foot. If this Volla is the Scandinavian Fulla, she was known in Germany. She may have been a goddess of abundance, as her name denotes.

Of some of the goddesses named by Snorri, little or nothing is known. Saga dwells at Sokkvabekkr, a great abode. In *Grimnismal* she and Odin are said to drink from the waters there in cups of gold. She has been thought to be a form of Frigg. Eir is the healer and in *Svipdagsmal* she is named as one of the maidens of Mengloth, who seems to be a goddess of healing and also perhaps a form of Frigg. All that is known of Sjofn is that she turns the thoughts of men and women to love. Lofn is kind to those who call upon her, winning Odin's or Frigg's permission for men to come together in marriage. Var hears oaths made between men and women and takes vengeance on perjurers. Vör is wise and nothing can be hid from her. Syn keeps the door of the hall, shutting it before those who should not go in. At trials, i.e., at the Thing, she is a defence against suits which she wishes to refute. Hlyn protects those whom Frigg desires to save from danger. Snotra is prudent and of gentle bearing. Gna is sent by Frigg over lands on her messages, her steed being Hoof-tosser, running over sea and sky.

Sol was sister of the moon, Mani, and they were children of Mundilfari, and the gods, angry with him for giving them these names, placed them in the sky, Sol to drive the horses and chariot of the sun, made by the gods from glowing fire from Muspellheim, and Mani to steer the course of the moon, arranging its waxing and waning. There seems to be some confusion here between sun and moon and the drivers of their chariots. In *Vafthruthnismal* Sol and Mani, children of Mundilfari, are sun and moon, the first making the round of the sky by day, the other by night so that men might know the time. The wolves Skoll and Hati are ever pursuing the sun and moon, to devour them, possibly a reference to eclipse myths.

Nanna was the consort of Balder, dying of grief at his death, and going with him to the underworld, Hel. Sigyn was Loki's wife, and mother of Narfi and Vali. In Snorri's account, Loki, taken by the gods, probably after causing Balder's death, was bound with the intestines of Narfi, who had been torn asunder by Vali, transformed into a wolf by the Æsir. *Lokasenna* makes Narfi the wolf, and Vali him by whose intestines Loki is bound. A venomous serpent was set over Loki's face, so that its venom would fall upon him. Sigyn held a shell under the drip of venom, but whenever she emptied it some poison fell on Loki, and his struggles were then the cause of earthquakes, one form of a frequent myth that earthquakes are the result of the movements of a monstrous being.

Two goddesses, not numbered among the Asynjur, Thorgerd and Irpa, are regarded by some as of Finnish origin. They were worshipped chiefly in Halogaland. There were several temples sacred to them. In one, described in *Njal's Saga*, their images stood beside that of Thor, life-sized and wearing amulets. They were regarded as having power over some parts of nature, especially causing tempests and hail when besought to do this. One of their worshippers, Hako, a jarl, prayed for their help against the Jomsvikings, but only when he had sacrificed his son did he gain success, the enemy being wasted with hail and storm. Hropp took armlets and rings from all three images and burned their temple. On discovering this Hako said that Hropp would never reach Valhall.

Ran was a sea-goddess, wife of the sea-god Ægir. She had a net with which she drew down those who went by sea or were drowning. Her claws are also spoken of. The sea was called "the land of Ran." The waves flow forth from her mouth. On the whole she was regarded as harmful, representing the sea in its dangerous aspect, yet apparently the drowned fared well in her sea-hell. In the *Eyrbyggia Saga* certain drowned men appeared at their burial feast, dripping with sea-water. This was considered a good sign of their happiness with Ran. The phrase "to fare to Ran" meant to be drowned at sea. Ran's daughters were nine in number, their names showing that they were the waves personified, the waves which wash the heads of the Norse ships and seek to sink them— "the horses of the sea." In *Baldrs Draumar* it is said that they will weep at his death and in their grief toss the ships up to the sky. Of a worship of Ran nothing is known except that human victims sacrificed before a voyage may have been offered to her (p. 146).

Snorri includes among the Asynjur Jörd (Earth), mother of Thor by Odin, and Rindr, Vali's mother, by Odin. Hence they are called co-wives of Frigg.

Of all these lesser goddesses or of their worship, if any was paid to them, much less is recorded than of the greater goddesses, e.g., Frigg and Freyja.

CHAPTER IV

LESSER SUPERNATURAL BEINGS

THE Norse Alfar or elves (sing. Alfr) had apparently an importance which is not clearly defined in the sources, for they are classed with the Æsir, as in the phrase "Æsir ok Alfar," as in a similar Anglo-Saxon phrase *esa* and *ylfe*. The word probably originally meant "spirits." They are mentioned with the Æsir, as in a passage of *Fafnismal* in the Poetic Edda, where the Norns are said to be kin to gods, elves, and the dwarf Dvalin, and in the account of Doom in *Voluspa* it is said, "how fares it with the Æsir, how fares it with the Alfar?" In the *Hrafnagaldr* they are classed with Æsir and Vanir, Alfar have skill, Vanir knowledge.

In Scandinavian mythology, as is stated in Snorri's Edda, Alfheim is the home of the Light-elves, Ljösalfar, which is also the abode of the god Frey, who is thus their chief. The Light-elves are fairer than the sun. Nothing is known of their origin. While the Eddic poems know only of one group of Alfar, Snorri speaks also of Dark Elves, whose abode is in the earth, and who are darker than pitch, unlike the others in nature. He names also the Black Elves, and tells how Odin sent Skirnir to their region to certain dwarfs, who then made the magic fetter Gleipnir to bind the Fenris wolf. The suggestion is that Dark and Black Elves and dwarfs belong to one group.

Whether worship was paid to the Ljösalfar is far from clear, but in the *Kormak's Saga* there would seem to be some trace of it, though the Alfar there mentioned dwell in a hill. In order that Thordis might obtain healing of his wounds, on this hill was to be poured the blood of a bull and a feast of its flesh was to be made for the Alfar. It is possible that the Alfar here are souls of the dead, living in their burial-mound. An *alfablot*, or sacrifice to the Alfar, was performed in the houses of still pagan folk after the introduction of Christianity, but its nature is not described.

In Iceland the nearest later approach to the Alfar are elfin folk called also Alfar and Huldu, "hidden folk," or by the euphemism Liuflingar, "darlings." They do not fear the light, like most elfin beings, though in *Hamthesmal* the dawning sun is called "the sorrow of Alfar," perhaps a late interpolation, as in *Alvismal* the Alfar are said to call the sun "fair wheel." These Icelandic elves dwell in rocks and hills and have similar traits to fairies and elves elsewhere. In one form or another and under various names elves are known over the whole Teutonic area, as beings dwelling underground or in hillocks, now friendly, now hostile to men, like our own fairies.

For full information about later elves of all kinds see Grimm, *Teutonic Mythology*, Chap. 17, and T. Keightley, *Fairy Mythology*.

The dwarfs (*dvergar*) are spoken of in the Eddas, and we learn how the first of them were created (p. 154). A long list of their names is given by Snorri. They were known from early times among all Germanic peoples, as underground dwellers, especially skilled in metal-work, though other ingenious things are ascribed to them in the Eddas. One group called Ivaldi's sons made hair of gold for Sif, Thor's wife, when Loki had cut off her hair ; Frey's boar, which could run through air and water and gave a bright light ; Thor's hammer which never failed to strike and, when he threw it, returned to his hand; Odin's spear Gungnir, which never failed in its thrust; the ship of the gods, Skidbladnir, which would always have a favouring breeze and which could be folded up like a napkin and put in Frey's pocket ; and Odin's gold ring, Draupnir, from which eight rings of the same weight would drop every ninth night.

Swords of magic power and other weapons and armour were made by dwarfs, e.g., Dainslef, Högni's sword, which caused death every time it was drawn and never failed in its stroke. A scratch made by it never healed. They made Gleipnir, the famous fetter, out of things which had no existence, e.g., the noise which a cat makes in walking, the breath of a fish, the spittle of a bird. It was soft and smooth, but even the Fenris-wolf could not break it.

Two dwarfs, Fjalar and Galarr, slew the man Kvasir, shaped by the gods out of their spittle, so wise that he could answer all questions. His blood was run into two vats and a kettle and blended with honey. This became mead of such quality that he who drank it became a skald. Hence poetry was called "the dwarf's drink."

Four dwarfs were placed by the gods at the four sides of heaven to support it where it joins earth. Hence heaven was called "the burden of the dwarfs" or "the helmet of Nordri, Sudri, Austri, and Vestri." (North, South, East and West.)

A huge stone in Sweden was the dwelling of a dwarf. Svegdir had gone to seek Odin, and, while intoxicated, came to this stone and saw sitting at it the dwarf, who bade him enter and he would find Odin. But the door of the stone shut behind him and he never came forth again. At the Doom of the gods the dwarfs are described as "groaning before their stone doors."

These dwarfs of the early Scandinavian literature, dwellers in rocks or under the earth, skilled artificers, owners of treasure, are continued in the various dwarfs, *Unterirdische*, etc., of later Scandinavian and of Teutonic folk-tradition, of whom many tales were told. No worship is spoken of as paid to the dwarfs.

Trolls, a name now given to dwarfs in the North, or even as in Orkney, to fairy-like beings called *trows*, are much more harmful than dwarfs in the early literature. They are evil, akin to sorcerers and witches, and Thor is often said to have gone east to fight against them. One of the kennings for Thor was "slayer of giants and troll-women." The name troll was applied to any abnormal and undesirable being, and troll-women are often mentioned. One of these was seen riding a wolf with snakes for a bridle. Bragi saw one late at night in a forest. Such troll-women dwelt in the forest called Ironwood, and were called Ironwood-women. In the *Grettis Saga* a huge troll-woman came to Grettir's house, and a fierce fight between them followed. After hours of struggle she was drawing him to a deep river when he got his right hand free, drew his sword and cut off her arm, and she fell into the flood. (For stories of alter dwarfs and trolls, see T. Keightley, *Fairy Mythology*.)

Vættir generally appear as guardians of the land, spirits who are more or less bound to it and keep it from disaster. Thus when a wizard was sent to bring a report on Iceland to King Harald, he saw the land full of land-spirits, who took means to drive him off. In another story of Iceland a man took land where none had ever been able to settle because of the *land-vættir*. These *land-vættir* were generally harmless and kindly, but men were careful not to drive them from the land, lest it should suffer. It was a law that before coming in sight of land the figure-head of a ship should be removed, lest it should frighten the *land-vættir* with its gaping head and yawning jaws. In one story a woman endowed with second-sight saw the *land-vættir* following men. The name *vættir* had sometimes a wider application and might be applied to other groups of beings. Occasionally *vættir* or some kinds of them might be harmful if men were careless of their existence. No worship seems to have been paid to them or is not referred to. In one form or another they continued in later folk-tradition in Scandinavia.

The *fylgja* or "follower" bears something of the same relation to the individual as the *vættir* do to the land and its people. It was a kind of double or spirit-guardian of a person, to be seen by those with second sight, but often appearing in animal form, the animal bearing some relation to the character of the person whose *fylgja* it was, and ceasing to be when he died. In one poem Helgi is said to have several "followers," but this is unusual. There was a *fylgja* which had female form, the *fylgjukona*. In *Vigaglum's Saga*, Glum dreamt that a woman of vast size came walking up from the sea towards his house. When he woke he explained the dream as signifying the appearance of his grandfather's *fylgjukona*, for as she was beyond human height, so was he beyond men in good qualities, and that he must have died. This *fylgjukona* is described by Glum in verse as if she were a Valkyrie, as indeed are other similar spirit guardians. The *fylgjukona* appeared before a death in a family, and usually passed to another member of the family after the owner's death. The *fylgja* still survives in folk-tradition under that or some other name.

The Valkyries are Odin's war-maidens or choosers of the slain, just as Odin himself and Freyja (perhaps here a mistake for Frigg, Odin's consort) are said to choose those who have fallen in battle, half chosen by the god, half by the goddess. One of Odin's names was Val-father, "father of the slain," as he received the warriors whom these choosers of the slain brought to Valhall. They were also called "battle-maids" or "helmet-maids" or "wish-maidens"—fulfillers of Odin's wishes. While they are minor goddesses, mortal maidens might be raised to their rank, like Brunhild. Sent by Odin, they rode forth to battle wearing helmets. There they called men's fates and gave victory, but the slain they brought to Valhall. There they, Herjan's maids (Herjan is Odin) attend the service of the table, bring the horn of wine to Odin, and serve the warriors with ale. A vivid picture of the Valkyries is found in *Eiriksmal*. Odin is described as waking from a dream in which he had seen a hero, King Eirik, coming to Valhall, and had ordered seats to be prepared with vessels of ale and had bidden the Valkyries make ready the wine. This is followed by the actual appearance of the King with others, making a great clamour. Odin bids Sigmund and Sinfjotli go forth to meet them, and the god looks eagerly for this fighter in many lands. Another picture is found in the *Hakonarsmal*. Two Valkyries had been sent forth by Odin. Hako is dying on the battlefield. He hears the Valkyries as they ride with shield and helmet, and learns how he and many more are about to enter Valhall. Enquiring why victory had not been his, Hako learns that the enemy are in flight, and that now he and the slain are to be guests in Valhall, a great access to the army of the gods.

Differing lists of the names of Valkyries are given in *Voluspa* and *Grimnismal* in the Poetic Edda, and the former names one of them Skuld, the third of the Norns. Snorri names her with two others, Gudr and Rota, specially as taking the slain and giving victory.

The Valkyries are described as wearing swords, carrying spears, their byrnies red with blood, riding over air and sea. Sometimes they go in groups of nine. In the Eddic poem *Helgakvitha Hjorvarthssonar* Helgi saw nine Valkyries riding, of whom the fairest, Svava, gave him his name and told him where to find a magic sword on which runes and a snake were engraved. Of this he gains possession. Svava shielded him often in battle. In another poem Helgi saw Sigrun (who is

Svava, a human Valkyrie, reborn) riding through the air with eight other Valkyries when he was at sea in a great storm, which now abated. Three groups of nine are also spoken of. One of them rode before the others. From their horses' manes came dew which fell in the valleys and hail on the woods. Kites and ravens are the birds of the Valkyries because they feed on the slain.

One aspect of the Valkyries is that some of the heroines of the Eddic poems are so-called, whether myth raised them to that rank, or they were confused with Valkyries called by their names. Svava was one of these, and she was re-born as Sigrun, while a Valkyrie, Kara, is said to be a re-birth of Sigrun. In the form of a swan she flew over Helgi, protecting him, but his sword swung so high that he caused her death. Brynhild, daughter of Buthli, is called a Valkyrie. Sigurd rode up a mountain girt with flames. There was a tower of shields, within which lay one sleeping in armour, whom he found to be a woman, a Valkyrie. Her name was Sigrdrifa. She had slain Hjalmgunna in battle, when Odin had promised him victory, and for this Odin, in anger, pierced her with a "sleep-thorn" as a punishment, and said that she would never win victory in battle and would be married. Sigrdrifa was Brynhild. She speaks of herself as a swan-maid, and other Valkyries are also so described, like those in the *Völundrkvitha*, who are said to be of human birth. The name Svanhild expresses the combination of swan-maid and Valkyrie, since it means "swan-maid warrior."

The Valkyrie belief was much developed in the north in Viking times, like that in Valhall. It may have come there from southern Germany, "the southern maid" being an occasional epithet for a Valkyrie. It is also possible that the idea of mythical Valkyries may have originated from the fact that, among the Germanic tribes, actual women went forth to battle. These are mentioned in the Poetic Edda where, in *Atlakvitha* they are called *skjaldmeyjar*, "shield-maids," many of whom perished in the temple of Atli. Saxo Grammaticus also speaks of such women more than once. They took part in the battle of Bravalla on the side of the Danes.

The Nial's Saga, describing the battle of Clontarf in 1014,

gives a horrible picture of a weaving by Valkyries. Dörradr saw twelve women riding to a bower. Looking in through a crevice he saw them weaving. The weights of the loom were human heads, warp and woof were human entrails, spools were swords, arrows the reel. The women sang a song describing these, and how the battle would go on while they stood by the side of the Norsemen and their King, and would have care of the slain. They called themselves Valkyries. The song ended, they divided into two bands, one riding north, one south.

This is not unlike the dream of Glum in *Viga-Glum's Saga*. He saw two women with a trough who sprinkled all the district with blood. This portended a battle in which these "maids of carnage," grim and vengeful, would, as the battle raged, "drench the land in slaughtered warriors' blood." Both descriptions give a cruder conception of the Valkyries than that in the Eddas.

Another late glimpse of the Valkyries is found in Saxo Grammaticus. In his version of the Balder story, he tells how Hotherus found certain wood-maidens, *virgines sylvestres*, who told him that they decided the issues of war, assisted in battle those to whom they were friendly and gave them victory. This is clearly a late tradition of the Valkyries, though erroneously regarding them as spirits of the woodland.

The Norns are an embodiment of the belief in Fate which was of great importance in Scandinavian religion, mythology, and life. Fate was so profound a conception that even the gods were subject to it, and could not escape it, and as a line in the *Atlamal* says, "No one can avoid his fate." Fate is not unknown in other religions, e.g., in Greek and Roman, where the belief in *moira* and *fatum* had a considerable influence, issuing in the conception of Moirai or Parcae.

Sometimes three Norns are spoken of, or, again, three separate bands, or sometimes several. Thus *Voluspa* tells of three dwelling in a hall under the tree Yggdrasil, Urd, Verdandi, and Skuld—Past, Present, and Future, the two latter names perhaps coined by a later interpolator, Urd actually meaning "Weird." They allot life to men and set their fates. Urd is connected with German *wurt*, Anglo-Saxon *wyrd*, in the sense of "fate," and it is continued in "the weird sisters" of Macbeth, from Holinshed, wielders of destiny. In *Vafthruthnismal* there are three groups or throngs of maidens, Norns, of giant race, who protect men, and in *Fafnismal* the Norns are said to be of different descent, some sprung from the Æsir, some from *alfar*, some from Dvalin, chief of dwarfs. These are probably of lesser importance than the three chief Norns.

That Norns influenced the destiny of the gods seems implied in *Voluspa*. The gods dwelt in peace, playing at tables, perhaps a kind of chess, and having no lack of gold. Then came three giant maids out of Jötunheim, and apparently their coming had serious consequences for the gods. Snorri paraphrases the stanza, saying that this was the age of gold for the gods before it was spoiled by the coming of the women from Jötunheim. These giant women are assumed to be the three Norns, here said to be of giant race. Their coming led eventually to the Doom of the gods.

The three who dwell under Yggdrasil by Urd's well made laws and allotted life to men. These they scored on wood in magic runes. Snorri speaks of them as determining the periods of human lives, coming to each child's birth to appoint its life, but he adds that there are many Norns. This is in *Gylfaginning* where many matters are explained to Gylfi by the gods. He objects that if Norns allot the fates of men they do this in an uneven way, for some have a pleasant life, others have not, some long life, some short. But Har (Odin) explains that Norns of good and honourable life allot good, but there are evil Norns who allot evil fortune. *Fafnismal* speaks of Norns helpful in need who bring the babe from its mother.

As an example of Norns allotting fates to men the poem *Helgakvitha Hundingsbana* tells how, at the birth of Helgi, Norns came and shaped his life. He was to be a famous fighter, and best of princes. Thus they wove for him the golden threads of fate. The threads were laid to the east and west and to the north, an indication of the spread of Helgi's future fame. The Norns are here represented as appearing visibly. The fate of the Norns, says *Fafnismal*, is strong in youth's voyage and danger looms then. But none may avert his fate. No man can war with the words of Urd, or fate, though she gives gifts where they were not earned, says *Svipdagsmal*, but her bolts on every side will be man's guard on life's way.

But the decrees of the Norns sometimes seemed evil to men, hence the epithets "cruel," "evil," "ill," are applied to them. Atli told how the Norns had wakened him from sleep by the terrible dreams which they sent him. Sigurd was told by Odin in the form of an old man called Hnikar that *talar-disir*, evil goddesses, a phrase here used for the Norns, would be at both his sides, unseen, when he went to fight, willing him to receive wounds. Norns drove Hamther to kill a hero and he blames them for this, but none can outlive the time ordained by them. Gudrun's heart was sore for the wrath of the Norns, and she tried to escape this by drowning, but the sea cast her ashore and she must live longer. Wolves are called the hounds of the Norns.

In the *Nornagest's Saga* an interesting picture is given of women, *volvur* or *spâkonur* who foretell fates, and this suggests that actual spaewives or soothsaying women may have helped to give rise to the belief in mythical fate-giving Norns. This is supported from other examples of the doings of such women. The Saga described three *spâkonur* or Norns, such as were invited to houses, fed, and given gifts. Three came to the house where the child Nornagest was in his cradle. Two of them said that he would be greater than any of his kindred or sons of chiefs. The third, who had been pushed off her seat, said in anger that he would live only so long as the candle lit beside him should burn. The eldest of the three blew out the candle, and giving it to his mother, bade her not to re-light it till the day of her son's death. The three then received gifts and went away. The story is late, of the fourteenth century, and may have been influenced by that of Meleager and the Parcae, yet it is but one example of the doings of such spaewives.

On the other hand a story told by Saxo Grammaticus says that it was an ancient custom to consult the oracles of the Parcae, i.e., Norns, regarding the fate of children. Fridlevus, desirous of discovering that of his son Olave, solemnly made vows and approached the temple of the gods. Looking into the sanctuary, he saw three nymphs seated. The first bequeathed to the child a gracious form and high place in human favour, the second the gift of generosity. The third, in envious mood, affixed the fault of parsimony to his character. The Norns are represented as sitting in a temple. Possibly their images are intended, but, if so, it is not clear how they ordained the future of the child.

Both stories illustrate the widespread medieval tradition of three spaewives or fairies who tell fortunes or fates, the third usually giving an evil fate, contrary to what the others do.

In a verse known as the Merseburg charm, from a tenth century document preserved at Merseburg, and possibly of earlier date, certain Idisi, one group fastening bonds on prisoners taken, another holding back the enemy, a third breaking the fetters of prisoners held in the enemy's camp, are spoken of. These Idisi are like the Norse *disir*, a word applied to goddesses, Norns and Valkyries, also to spirits of the dead. If the Idisi are a kind of Valkyries the conception of war-maids may have been known to Germanic tribes. *Disir* also appears in the word *spadisir*, corresponding to *spâkonur*. Disir are now friendly, now hostile like the *talar-disir*, evil Norns, already spoken of. There is occasional mention of a *disablot*, a sacrifice to the *disir*. This suggests that sacrifices may have been made to the Norns as well as other female supernatural beings, and such a sacrifice may have been the object of Fridlevus' vows.

The well of Urd, which is very holy, is under one of the roots of the ash Yggdrasil, and is called by the name of the chief Norn. She and those dwelling with her sprinkle the tree daily with water from the well to prevent its rotting or withering.

CHAPTER V

NATURE AND BEINGS DERIVED FROM IT

THE worship of nature, of sky, sun, earth, sea, rivers, mountains, trees, or of the spirits of these, has been widespread, and we have seen it as it existed among the Celts. From this primitive worship, from the belief that the different parts of nature are living entities, that spirits of these existed, and from men's early worship of them, arose by successive steps the idea of the greater deities, still connected with the parts of nature from which they sprung. But certain parts of nature were still associated with various spirits, who might be friendly or otherwise to man, and whom he took care to propitiate.

Nothing is more common in primitive myth, surviving into higher stages, than the idea that heaven and earth are a divine pair from whom all things proceed. If Odin (Woden) in the earlier stages of Teutonic religion was a sky-god, this would explain why he is constantly said to be consort of Jörd, Earth personified. Jörd was counted among the Asynjur or goddesses, and she is sometimes called Fjorgyn. How Jörd was worshipped is not known, but some folk-customs may continue that worship. The importance of Mother Earth is seen in what Tacitus says of the goddess Nerthus, worshipped by some Germanic tribes. He calls her Mother Earth and describes her functions and worship (p. 96).

The sun, Sol, was female, and Snorri includes her among the Asynjur. She must have been an object of worship from early times, but the myths about her and the Moon throw no light on this, though some worship of her existed, as medieval ecclesiastical documents condemn it. From early times the sun was symbolized by a disc or wheel, and a bronze disc representing the sun, set on a chariot with six wheels, on the axles of the first four of which stands a horse, was found in Iceland some years ago. According to Snorri, horses draw the chariot of the sun and this might be connected with the bronze relic, save that the horse itself is also on the wheels. In all probability the bonfires in Scandinavia, at early or mid-summer, as among the Celts and elsewhere in Europe, were lit to aid the sun in its progress—a magical rite.

Waters—wells, rivers, the sea—had here as elsewhere a divine aspect. The cult of waters by the Germanic tribes is often mentioned, and there is little doubt that it existed also in Scandinavia. We shall see later that in close proximity to a sacred grove there was often a sacred pool of water or a well. The sacredness of wells is everywhere known, their healing properties, especially where they were medicinal. From the sacred spring of Fosite in Heligoland, water was drawn in silence, and death was the penalty of profaning it. The sacred fountains in Scandinavian regions were even transferred to divine regions. The well of Mimir, who was full of old lore, the well in which wisdom was kept, was under one of the roots of the world-tree Yggdrasil. Under another root was the well of Urd, which was "very holy," its waters sprinkled on the tree to preserve it.

The sacredness of water is seen from the fact that soon after a child's birth it was sprinkled with water by the father. This gave the child a full status among the kin. There is reference to this in *Havamal*, the speaker mentioning that the sprinkling would later preserve the child from falling in battle. Other notices occur in the Sagas. The washing of the chariot of Nerthus in a lake after the procession of the goddess is described by Tacitus. Oaths were sworn beside streams, showing their sacredness.

The sea had its spirits or deities, Ran, Ægir, their nine daughters, the waves, as has been seen.

There were spirits of the waters, helpful, or harmful, which are mainly known from folk-survivals or in tradition. In the poem of *Beowulf* there are described the harmful water beings, Grendel and his mother, a *merewif*. Grendel dwells in a lake overshadowed by trees, in the gloomy fen ; his mother in a hall far below the water. In his thirst for blood Grendel attacks human beings. Here, too, *niceras* are said to dwell. This word is akin to the English *nix*, *nixie*, in old Norse *nykr*, with corresponding forms in later Norse, Swedish, and Danish.

The Norse *nök* is also known as *soetrold*. The male is old, dwarfish, or, as in Iceland and Sweden, he may appear as a horse or as a fish. In the latter form he may be compared to the dwarf Andvari in the Poetic Edda, who dwelt in the water as a pike. The *nök* assumed a youthful form to entice girls. The Icelandic *nykr*, as a horse, tempted someone to mount him and then rushed into the water. Though thus dangerous, the souls of the drowned were kept by him in his water realm, just as the sea-goddess Ran drew them to her by means of her net.

The female nixies were beautiful and, like mermaids, were seen combing their long tresses. Their sweet songs beguiled unwary youths who were drawn into the waters. These nixies are but little distinguished from mermaids, in old Norse *haf-fru*, with a male form *marmennill*, who had prophetic gifts.

All these are later representatives of similar water beings of the pagan period.

The forests, vast and wide, were mysterious and easily peopled with spirits more or less dangerous. Certain trees and groves were sacred among the Teutonic tribes, and this was so also in Scandinavia. The grove, as with the Celts, was the earliest temple, and even when temples came into existence, sacred groves still remained, beside them, sacrificial victims being hung on the trees. Individual trees were honoured for their vast size or as the dwelling of a spirit or deity. In later times the belief in spirits haunting the forest continued, even if these were given other forms or names. The spirit animating a tree always tended to be separable from it, and as there were many trees in a forest, so there were many tree-spirits who appeared apart from them and to whom certain forms were ascribed. They generally had elfin traits. Certain wood women of a monstrous kind called *ividjur* are mentioned in the Poetic Edda; in *Hyndluljoth*. Snorri speaks of a forest called Ironwood, in which troll-women lived, probably woodland spirits of a harmful kind, but nothing definite is known of them. In his story of Balder and Hotherus, Saxo Grammaticus tells how the latter came upon a conclave of *virgines sylvestres*, woodland women, who gave him advice and then vanished. The Danish *skogsnufa*, forest-maidens, the Swedish *skogsrå*, wood-goblin, *skogsfru*, wood-wife, are examples of woodland fairy-like beings. A great variety of such wood-wives was known in Teutonic belief and literature. Danish and Swedish wood-wives have a semi-animal form or wear skins of animals. Some, if not all of these wood-folk are earlier tree-spirits. In Denmark the elder-mother dwelt in the elder-tree, and whoever would take part of it had to ask her permission, just as generally he who would fell a tree must first kneel before it with uncovered head and folded hands.

What precise worship was offered to the spirits of waters or trees is far from clear, but long after Christianity had been accepted some form of it continued, for the Church constantly tried to extirpate it. The words used in ecclesiastical prohibitions show that the kindling of lights, offerings, and prayers were used in these survivals. These, with whatever other ceremonies now disused, had been immemorial practices, existing before gods had assumed personal forms.

JÖTNAR, THURSAR

Giants, called by these names, appear prominently in Scandinavian mythology, and have been regarded as forms of an earlier savage race, overpowered by the incoming peoples, and transmuted into a monstrous, yet still human form. They have been also regarded, as by Grimm, as akin to the wild, hairy wood-sprites of Germanic tradition, though these are not of gigantic size. Perhaps it is better to look upon them as embodiments of the greater forces and aspects of nature— the frost, ice, snow of the northern regions, the mountains and huge rocks, the sea. This view has at least some connexion with the collective names under which they were grouped— *Hrimthursar*, Rime-giants, those of frost and snow, and *Bergrisi*, *Bergbui*, Hill-giants, the two divisions in which Snorri classes them. Sea-giants may be seen in Ægir, a personification of the sea in its calm state, and Hymir, of the *Hymiskvitha*, with his frozen beard, a giant of the icy sea. Thrymheim, the abode of the giant Thjazi, is on the mountains; other giants dwelt in hills. Jötunheim, the giants' abode, is perhaps among the mountains. Here giants have their separate abodes. They, like the gods, had a watchman, Eggther. Above him sat the cock Fjalar, who was to warn the giants by his crowing when the Doom of the gods arrived.

The giants' weapons were of stone, e.g., huge clubs. Hrungnir, whom Thor slew (his heart, head, and shield were of stone), had as weapon a hone. This was cast at Thor, whose hammer struck and broke it. From one part of it came all whinstone blocks.

A late but none-the-less illuminating genealogy of giants clearly points to their connexion with the forces of nature. Förnjot was father of the giants, of those whose early home was in Norway. His immediate sons were Wind, Fire (Logi), and Sea. Wind had a son, Glacier, and his son was Snow. Snow's children were Black Frost, Snow, Snow-heap, and Snow-drift. Among the giants at Utgard-loki's hall was Logi, Wild-fire, against whom Loki had to contend at eating. Before Loki could eat the meat from the bones, Logi had devoured meat and bones and the trough containing them. Snorri, following verses in the Poetic Edda, speaks of the origin of the giants, the first of whom was Ymir. From him sprang all the giants. He was formed from the meeting of warm air from Muspellheim and rime from Ginnunga-gap. This caused a kind of yeast in which life was quickened, and from this Ymir was produced. Under his left hand grew a male and female; one foot begat a son with the other. Odin, Vili, and Ve, of later origin than Ymir, slew him and created the world from different parts of his body. In his flowing blood all existing Rime-giants were drowned, save Bergelmir, the wise giant, and his wife, who escaped in a boat. From them sprang the later Rime-giants.

Some of the giants were of enormous size. Thor, with Thjalfi and Loki, went to Jötunheim and at night came to what seemed a huge hall with an opening as wide as the hall. There they stayed for the night, during which there was an earthquake. Thor and his companions found a side room where they sheltered. At dawn, Thor saw a vast man sleeping close by, whose movements had caused the earthquake. He woke, recognized Thor, and, stretching out his hand, took up his glove. This was the hall in which Thor and the others had sheltered, the side room being the thumb of the glove. In the *Lokasenna* Thor is taunted by Loki for having hidden in the thumb of a glove, as he also is by Odin in the flyting poem *Harbards ljoth*. A giantess, Gjalp, could straddle across two ravines.

Some giants were many-headed. The son of Ymir had six heads, the mother of Hymir nine hundred. A throng of many-headed giants is spoken of, as also are three-headed giants. Generally, the giants are stupid, but some possess great wisdom and are given the epithet "wise." Vafthruthnir is so wise that even Odin seeks him out to hear his wisdom, his knowledge of things past and to come, as is told in the Eddic poem *Vafthruthnismal*. Another giant, Suttung, possessed the mead of poetry, which Odin captured from him by means of various stratagems, so that now the Æsir have the gift of poetry.

Many giantesses are named and their beauty is dwelt on, and one had such attractions that Frey, seeing her, had a great lovesickness, and later married her. Other unions between gods and giantesses are mentioned, or between giants and goddesses, e.g., Njörd married Skathi, daughter of the giant Thjazi.

While giants are usually mild in temper, yet they are called fierce, and their wrath, *jötunmödi*, is easily roused and forces them to violent action. Hrungnir ran his horse, Gold-mane, against Odin's Sleipnir, and was so filled with giant rage that he galloped into Asgard where he became so drunk and boastful that he said he would carry all Asgard to Jötunheim, kill the gods, and take Sif and Freyja to him. Later he was killed by Thor.

The gods and the giants live in a kind of neutral attitude to each other, but the former take precautions against them. Thus Bifrost bridge, stretching from Asgard to earth, is guarded by the god Heimdall, lest the Hill-giants should attempt its passage. The gods' citadel was built to be proof against Hill- and Frost-giants. In spite of this, giants and gods sometimes adopt respectful attitudes to each other. Hill- and Frost-giants were present at Balder's funeral. It should be remembered also that Odin, Vili, and Ve are sons of a giant,

Borr, and a giantess Bestla. Hence they are spoken of in *Voluspa* as "Borr's sons." But when the giants become obstreperous Thor is their opponent and slays them, as many myths show. Snorri says of this that the giants know Thor's hammer, Mjöllnir, when it is raised on high, for it has bruised many of them, and was the chief defence against them. Frey, lacking his sword, slew the giant, Beli, with his fist. The hero Helgi slew the giant Hati, mightiest of giants, whom he found sitting on a mountain.

Surt, the Fire-giant, rules over Muspellheim. His wife is the giantess Sinmora. At the Doom of the gods, Surt comes forth with the sons of Muspell and burns up the world with fire. Sinmora possesses the sword which alone can slay the cock Vithofnir (probably the same as Gollinkambi), whose crowing wakes the gods when the time of Doom begins.

Many individual giants are named, some in connexion with Odin, but more with Thor's adventures. Thrym, the giants' leader, sat on a mound in Jötunheim, having stolen and hid Thor's hammer. In disguise as Freyja whom Thrym desired to wed, Thor was welcomed by him, and his hammer brought in to hallow the pretended bride. He seized it and slew Thrym and all the giants who were there. Others whom he combated are named, e.g., Thjazi, whose eyes he (or Odin in Snorri's version) threw up to heaven where they became stars. Gymir was father of Gerth whom Frey married. For the giantess Hyrrokin, the gods sent to launch Balder's funeral ship when they could not move it. With one thrust she pushed it out to sea.

Some giants had animal form. Two in particular are described, the Midgard serpent who encircles the ocean, or is perhaps a monstrous personification of the ocean ; and the horrible Fenris wolf, bound by the gods, but at their Doom he overcomes Odin. These are the offspring of the enigmatic Loki, himself son of the giant Farbauti and the giantess Laufey. These monstrous offspring were born to Loki by the giantess Angrbotha.

Giants could change their shape. The giantess Hrimgerth took that of a mare; the giant Thjazi that of an eagle. They had also the power of deception or causing illusion, as in the long story of Thor who was deluded by Skrymir or Utgard-Loki into thinking he had failed to empty a drinking-horn, or had been unable to raise one paw of his huge cat, or to wrestle successfully with the old woman Elli. Actually the end of the horn was in the sea, which had diminished by Thor's draught. The cat was the Midgard Serpent, which he had lifted from its place. Elli was Old Age, who had caused him to fall on his knee. Moreover Utgard-Loki and his castle vanished when Thor was about to strike him with his hammer after he had explained these illusions.

ANIMALS

The gods possessed horses, on which they daily rode over Bifrost to hold council, Thor alone walking. A list of their names is given in both Eddas, but only two of their owners are named. Odin owned Sleipnir, eight-legged, the best of horses. The origin of this steed is curious. The giant artificer who built a citadel for the gods was helped by his stallion Svadilfari. In order to prevent his getting the reward for which he had asked, when the work was all but done Loki turned himself into a mare which attracted the stallion and the work was unfinished within the time agreed upon. Loki, as a mare, gave birth to Sleipnir. The other owner of a steed who is named is Heimdall. It was called Gulltop, "Gold-topped." Heimdall himself was called Gullintani, "Gold-toothed," because his teeth were of gold.

Some horses were sacred to the gods. In an account of the destruction of an image of Frey by King Olaf, the horses consecrated to the god were found grazing in the precincts of his temple. The horse was a frequent sacrificial animal and its head was fastened to a tree. Sometimes a horse's head was fixed on a stake, the *neidstang*, with the jaws made to gape open. This was expected to do harm to an enemy if he came near it.

Cattle, besides being sacrificial victims, were also sometimes sacred to a deity, grazing on his land and not to be touched, like those of Fosite in Heligoland. Cattle also drew the car with the image of Nerthus. There are occasional notices of a cow regarded as sacred and worshipped, and taken everywhere with its owner.

The boar, besides being offered in sacrifice, was sacred to Frey. His own boar, Gullinbursti, "gold bristles," was made by dwarfs, and on it he rode. A periodical sacrifice of a boar was made to Frey and was called *sônar-göltr* or "atonement-boar." Cakes in the shape of a boar were eaten at the midwinter festival. Amulets made in the likeness of a boar were worn.

The cat was sacred to Freyja, who drove in a chariot drawn by cats, e.g., when she went to Balder's funeral. Hence the epithet given to her, "possessor of the gib-cats."

Other animals were connected with the gods. Odin had two wolves, Geri and Freki, to whom he gave all his meat at the divine banquets, for he lived on wine alone. These wolves were called his hounds. Two ravens, Huginn, "Thought," and Muninn, "Memory," perched one on each of Odin's shoulders after they had gone about the world since dawn at his command. At night they told into his ears all they had heard and seen. Possibly these ravens are those which, as told in *Olaf Tryggvison's Saga*, when Hakon offered a great sacrifice, came croaking overhead, their presence, as Hakon supposed, a proof that Odin had accepted his offering and would give him victory. In another Saga it is said of a flight of ravens that they are Odin's messengers.

Freyja had hawk's plumage and could use it for flying, and so could anyone to whom she lent it. Frigg had similar plumage, which Loki used. Hence Frigg was known as "Mistress of the hawk-plumage."

The form of an eagle was sometimes assumed. Winds were caused by the giant Hraesvelg, who, in the shape of an eagle, sat at the edge of heaven on the eagle's hill, and by the movement of his wings sent the winds over the world. Odin assumed the form of an eagle when he fled with the mead of poesy belonging to the giant Suttung, who pursued him, also in eagle's form. The giant Thjazi took the form of an eagle when he forced Loki to bring him the goddess Idunn and her apples of immortality.

In one of the Eddic poems, *Helgakvitha Hjorvarthssonar*, a wise bird twittered and spoke to Atli, and said that he would tell him more if an offering was made to him, a temple and altars, with cattle whose horns were gilded. This bird is obviously a deity, who has taken that form.

The cock was associated with the gods and with giants. Gollinkambi, called also Vithofnir, sits on the tree Yggdrasil, and by his crowing, awakes the gods and warriors to prepare for the Doom of the gods. The cock Fjalar sits ready to awake the giants for that same time.

Swans were mainly important from the belief in Swan-maidens, supernatural women who possessed swan-garments which they doffed, appearing as beautiful women, or put on and flew away. They were captured if these swan-garments were obtained, but, if at any time they recovered them they flew off from their human captors. Some Valkyries appeared as Swan-maidens, as may be seen in the Eddic poem *Völundarkvitha*, and are captured, but the belief in such beings is world-wide and by no means confined to Scandinavia (see E. S. Hartland, *Science of Fairy-Tales*, ch. x, xi).

Snakes were venerated to some extent, and there is evidence, outside Scandinavia, that some of the Germanic tribes worshipped a snake. Odin turned himself into a serpent in order to creep through a hole in the rock of Suttung's abode to acquire the mead of poesy. He also took the names of the two snakes which gnaw the twigs of the tree Yggdrasil, Ofnir and Svafnir, for what purpose is not told. Snakes were carved on swords in order to increase their power, and set on the crests of helmets, adding to their invulnerability. In *Kormak's Saga* Kormak was lent a famous sword and told how to draw it. A little snake would creep from under the hilt and creep back again. He did not follow the instructions and the sword lost its power. In the version of the Balder story given by Saxo Grammaticus the venom of three snakes drops on his food. This was intended to increase his strength when he ate the food. The story of the dwarf Andvari's treasure, which became that of the Nibelungs, tells of a snake or dragon. Loki killed the brother of Regin and Fafnir, Ottar, who had taken the shape of an otter. For this he, with Odin and Hœnir, had to fill the otter's skin with gold. Loki procured the gold from Andvari and it was given to Hreithmar, father of Regin and Fafnir. These now asked their father for a share of the gold, but he refused, and was slain by Fafnir. Going to the heath with the gold he turned himself into a snake or dragon and curled himself round it. By use of a magic sword Sigurd slew Fafnir in this shape. Regin, who had accompanied him, cut out Fafnir's heart and bade Sigurd roast it. Sigurd put his finger to it to see if it were cooked, burnt his finger and put it to his mouth. Now he understood the speech of birds. (*Reginsmal* and *Fafnismal* in Poetic Edda.) That dragons or snakes guard treasure is a widespread belief, but the point to note here is that secret knowledge is the result of eating the dragon's heart, which Regin had intended for himself. This is based on the belief that certain serpents possess wisdom or supernatural knowledge. If part of such a reptile is eaten that knowledge passes to the eater. Comparable with this is the story of Fionn and the salmon of knowledge (p. 50).

Grimm speaks of a traditional belief in house-snakes, usually connected with children, which it was unlucky to kill. They liked milk or were fed with it, a kind of offering. Traditions about such snakes suggest that the soul might appear as a snake, or that the dead appear in that form.

The myth of the tree Yggdrasil names the serpents which gnaw its twigs, and tells of a vast reptile, Nidhogg, which, along with several others, eats its roots. Nidhogg is also said to suck the blood of the slain, of two kinds of dire criminals, the treacherous and murderers, in the lower world.

CHAPTER VI

WORSHIP AND ITS ACCESSORIES

In speaking of the deities we have noted some references to
their temples. In his account of the Germanic tribes Tacitus
speaks of groves or sacred woods consecrated for worship;
on the other hand, describing the sacred grove of Nerthus,
he mentions her temple, and also that of Tamfana among the
Marsi. In the Scandinavian area such sacred groves existed,
but also many temples are mentioned in several places, though
a temple had often a sacred grove close to it. The names given
to temples were *hof*, *höll*, *blot-hus*. They were of wood, less
often of stone, some large, some small, even so small as to be
taken down and carried from Norway to Iceland. The *Eyrbyggia
Saga* describes one of many temples in Iceland, one of Thor's.
It was large, with a door in the side wall nearer to one end.
Within the door were the pillars of the high seat with the
"gods' nails" (a phrase not explained) upon them. Off the
main building, was another, like a chancel, with a stall or altar
upon which lay the ring on which oaths were sworn, and
which was worn on his arm by the chief at moots. On the
altar stood the blood-bowl for the blood of sacrificial victims,
and the sprinkler for sprinkling this. Round about the altar
were images of the gods. All men in the district paid toll to
the temple. Another large temple described in the *Kjalnesinga
Saga* was one hundred feet long, its width sixty feet. It had
curtains and windows. On the altar burned a perpetual fire.
The narrower extension of such temples, the more sacred
part, may have been more or less separate from the main
part. The ring on which oaths were sworn was reddened with
the blood of sacrificed animals. Human victims were sacrificed
outside the temple. The temple and its sacred area were
surrounded by a high fence.

   Iceland was divided into a number of districts, in each of
which there were temples. Temple-toll was paid to the *hof-
góthi* who presided over the temple and was also head of his

district and responsible for the temple's upkeep. The temple
was both a religious and political centre.

Temples in Norway were similar to those in Iceland. In
one of them the image of Thor was seated in a car. The images
of the deities in these temples were richly clothed, and had
gold and silver ornaments. Adam of Bremen describes the
great temple at Uppsala in Sweden. It was decked with gold
and was surrounded by a gleaming chain of gold. In it were
images of three deities, Thor with a sceptre seated in the
centre, on either side Odin, armed, and Frey. Beside the
temple was a sacred grove with a sacred tree, an ever-green,
with spreading branches. There was another important temple
at Lethra in Sweden.

Even in Iceland a temple might be richly adorned, like
one in which a rich settler told his sons to put a cross-beam of
silver on the temple which they were building, though they
refused.

There were many pagan temples in Saxon England before
its conversion to Christianity. The chief of King Edwin's
priests, Coifi, accepted the faith and said that he himself
would destroy the temple and images. To prove his abandon-
ment of paganism he rode a stallion; the heathen priest should
ride a mare only. Bearing a sword and spear, both unlawful
for a pagan priest to carry, he cast the spear into the temple,
profaning it. The people thought him mad, but he bade his
companions destroy by fire the temple, altars, images, and
sacred enclosure. This was at Godmenham, on the Derwent.
Unfortunately the historian Bede, who records this, does not
describe the temple.

The main part of a temple, apart from the more sacred
inner place with the images, was used for religious and other
gatherings, for the sacrificial feasts, for the taking of oaths—
the temple-oath in which the hand was laid on the ring already
spoken of. The notice from Bede suggests what careful
observance must be used by those who entered temples. On
Heligoland, a sacred island, if anyone profaned its temples he
was offered up as a sacrifice.

Images are not mentioned by Tacitus, but only certain
symbols of deities, but this need not rule out their existence

among the Germanic tribes. Sozomen speaks of a statue of a
deity which the Gothic tribes possessed, in his account of the
labour of Ulphilus among these. They did exist among the
Scandinavians, as some examples have shown. Some images
may have been made of gold, but mostly they were of wood,
and richly adorned. The *Nial's Saga* describes a Norwegian
temple with images of Thor and two female deities, Irpa and
Thorgerd, life-sized and wearing armlets. Other notices of
large images of Thor occur. Small images, chiefly of Thor,
were carried by worshippers. Each deity had his particular
attribute, e.g., Thor bore his hammer. On pillars beside the
high seat in the temples or houses heads of deities, Thor,
Odin, were carved. All images were systematically destroyed
by those who introduced Christianity or by their converts.
King Olaf went to the temple at Throndhjem where there were
several images, that of Thor being chief, adorned with gold
and silver. This he smote and it fell; the others were thrown
down by his followers.

There is frequent reference in different parts of the Teutonic
area, especially among the Saxons, to an *irminsul*, a grove, a
temple, but more particularly a lofty wooden pillar, originally
the trunk of a sacred tree. The word is translated by Rudolph
of Fulda as *universalis columna*, as if it sustained all things.
It may have represented a deity, but perhaps was a symbol
of the mythical world-pillar which sustained the sky. It was
held in great sanctity. It may be compared to great sacred
trees, like the oak of Jupiter (Thunar) at Hesse, which was of
unusual size.

Festivals and religious gatherings were held in late autumn
in connexion with harvest; at midwinter—Yule; in spring,
perhaps also at midsummer. At the harvest festival there was
a feast and sacrifice to the deities, and much merriment and
ale-drinking. The Yule feast lasted for three nights with much
ale-drinking. At all festivals sacrifices were offered, feasts
held, with drinking of toasts. Especially at the Yule festival
the dead were commemorated and were believed to be present,
taking part in the feast. But as is said in the *Ynglinga Saga*, the
festivals ordained by Odin had other purposes, that in autumn
when sacrifices were offered for a good year, at Yule for

growth, in summer for gain and victory. The festivals were times of peace; they united the people, and were occasions of great religious and social importance. Every nine years a great festival was held at Uppsala in Sweden and at Leire in Denmark. To the former all had to come and bring materials, and there were great sacrifices at both.

The participants in the festivals brought to the temples the sacrificial animals and victuals and all things needful for the common feasting. The blood (*hlaut*) of the animals was collected in the vessels kept in the temple for this purpose, and was sprinkled by means of the ceremonial sprinklers on the altar, the temple-walls inside and out, and the worshippers. The flesh of the sacrificed animals was cooked over fires within the temple and eaten by all present. The giver of the feast or the *góthi* had to bless the sacrificial meat and the toasts, and goblets of ale were passed over the fire before being drunk for special purposes—victory, plenty, peace, and in memory of the dead. Odin's toast was drunk for victory and the power of the King, Njörd's and Frey's for good seasons and peace. Bragi's toast was also sometimes drunk. The memory toast (*minne*) was drunk to kinsmen who had been laid in their barrows.

Sacrifice of things of greater or lesser value had been made from time immemorial. This was the chief way of showing dependence upon the deities, as well as of propitiating them in times of stress. In the Sagas, as showing the importance of sacrifice, it is often said that this or the other person was "a great sacrificer." Private sacrifices might be made by a worshipper at a sacred tree or well, to the spirit or deity connected with it, or to any particular god, the value of the sacrifice varying with the means or the need of the worshipper. But generally sacrifice was of a more social kind, offered by or on behalf of many, and followed by a joint feast on the flesh of the animals sacrificed, with libations offered and drunk to the well-being of gods or worshippers. At the festivals animals of various kinds were sacrificed, the horse being a common victim. The animals were provided by all the worshippers or by some prominent person. The sacrifices might be propitiatory or for thanksgiving, their purpose here as elsewhere was to establish a bond between the worshippers and the gods. A feast on the flesh of the victims followed, and the gods were supposed to be present invisibly feasting with their worshippers. While the sacrifice was the central act, other matters were involved at the festival gatherings, deliberations about public procedure, judicial affairs, buying and selling.

Sacrifices in Sweden were said to have been arranged by Frey himself, the sacrificial god of Sweden, and according to the *Ynglinga Saga*, which makes the gods men and kings, he raised the great temple at Uppsala, endowing it with his wealth. Bulls were offered to him, and libations poured forth, and toasts were drunk to him and to Njörd for fertility and peace. To the dead also their kinsmen sacrificed for a fruitful year. There are examples in the Sagas of sacrifices offered to heroic men after their death.

In Sweden the King is said to have given the largest boar available to Frey, whose animal it was. It was so holy that men swore over its bristles in great cases. It was sacrificed at Yule, when its head was brought into the hall before the King, and vows were made by pulling the hand over its bristles.

Human sacrifices had always been offered by the Teutons, as the witness of Tacitus and others shows, tò Woden and to Tyr, the war-god. Among the Scandinavians they were frequently offered, especially to Odin as war-god—prisoners, slaves, even women and children, and, if it was thought necessary, the victim was drawn from the community by the casting of lots. Procopius wrote of the northern people of Thule that they sacrifice to Ares, as greatest of the gods, the first prisoner taken. This they do by hanging him, or throwing him among thorns, or by some other cruel method. As Procopius wrote in the sixth century, Ares probably stands here for Odin. Persons who offended against society by some crime, or against the gods by sacrilege, were outside the law, and might be sacrificed as a propitiatory offering. In times of famine or other calamity, when the gods were presumed to be angry with their worshippers, human victims were offered to propitiate them. Even a King might then be sacrificed as the most valuable life in the land.

On one occasion as the sacrifices of oxen at Uppsala, and

next year of men, failed to cause increase in the land and famine prevailed, it was resolved to sacrifice Domald the King as it was believed that the scarcity had arisen because of him. The seats of the gods were reddened with his blood.

As life and its duration came from the gods, men sometimes offered a human victim in order to prolong their own lives. A passage in the *Heimskringla* tells of King Aunn of Uppsala sacrificing nine of his sons to Odin for this purpose, the god promising him so many years of continued life for each son.

The greatest offerings were those made for victory or after a victory, or even during the battle if victory seemed uncertain. Instances of this are given by Tacitus among the German tribes. In the Scandinavian area such sacrifices were made to Odin, as they had been to Tyr, and were on a large scale, especially in Denmark and Sweden.

Before sea voyages and warlike expeditions by sea human victims were offered on the shore. They may have been sacrificed to Thor, like those offered by the Norman Vikings before setting forth. But it is possible that they were offered to the sea-goddess Ran, to whom the drowned went.

At the nine years' festival at Uppsala in spring nine male victims, of men and animals, were offered to Frey and at the similar periodic festival at Leire ninety-nine men with horses, dogs, and cocks (in place of hawks) were sacrificed. This latter account is given by Dietmar of Merseburg a century after the festival had come to an end, and the numbers are probably exaggerated; the purpose of the sacrifice as stated by him— to aid the dead when they reach the other world and to placate for their sins—is probably an error. At Uppsala the heads and bodies of the victims, animal and human, were suspended from trees in the sacred grove beside the temple.

Beside some temples there were sacrificial pools in which human victims were sunk—the well of sacrifice. At Uppsala there was such a pool and when the victim did not rise to the surface this was considered as a sign that the prayers of the worshippers would be answered.

An interesting relic is described in the *Eyrbyggia Saga*, that of a "doom ring" in Iceland where men were doomed as victims, and within it Thor's stone on which they were broken, the stain of the blood being visible upon it.

The raiding Northmen had a horrible custom which added to the terror in which they were held, that of cutting "the bloody eagle" on the backs of their victims, apparently while still in life. Through this incision the vital parts were drawn out, the whole act combining revenge and sacrifice.

Sacrifice was accompanied by prayer to one or other of the gods to whom it was offered. The appropriate postures of the body or gestures were used, bowing the head before the image of the god, bending the body, uncovering the head, folding the hands, stretching out the hands. Little, however, is said of prayer. The words of Sigrdrifa in the Eddic *Sigrdrifumal* may be taken as an example of a prayer. She hails the day, the sons of day, and night, to grant victory; the gods and goddesses and the generous earth to give wisdom and speech and healing hands. Sometimes a token was asked to show that the prayer would be answered. Snorri says of Freyja that it is good to call on her for success in love, as it is good to call on Njörd for fruitfulness and peace. There is a curious stanza in *Havamal* which has been translated in different ways. Its meaning seems to be that no prayer at all is better than too large a sacrifice, and that better is no sacrifice than one that is too large, which recalls the higher prophetic teaching in the Old Testament about the Hebrew sacrifices and our Lord's words about vain repetitions.

At a moot when men made vows, these were taken on the temple ring with an oath, e.g., "So help me Frey and Njörd and the almighty Thor, as I pursue this suit and bear witness, etc."

Tacitus speaks of priests among the Germanic tribes, and apart from their sacred functions they had considerable power, like the Druids among the Celts. These priests, who acted in the name of a god, were guardians of the sacred groves and all connected with them. They carried into battle symbols and standards taken from the groves. They presided over divination. At public assemblies they demanded silence and had other powers at these. They judged offenders and ordered punishments. In Scandinavia, on the other hand, there are few references to priests as a separate body, though there are occasional notices of priests attached to a temple and offering sacrifices. But there appears to have been a union of priestly and political functions, though why this should have been is far from clear. Thus the king or a lesser political magnate, chief or jarl, not only was from his rank the chief person at political gatherings, he also offered the sacrifices and was conspicuous at the feast which followed. Thus when King Olaf became a Christian he went to Throndhjem and there the bonders desired him to offer sacrifice as other Kings had done before him. In Iceland the head of the *thing* or stated gathering of the people, the political leader of each district and head of the moot or meeting for justice, was responsible for the care of the temple and offered sacrifice, and took care of the consecrated ground where the *thing* met. He was called the *góthi*. This was true also of Sweden and Norway, where, however, the King had supreme political and priestly functions, offering sacrifices for the whole people. But the more local chiefs had also the joint office of *góthi*. This joint office, religious and civil, appears prominently in Iceland, where the chief settler in a district, who usually built a temple, became *góthi* of that district. Such men were sometimes called "friend of the god" or of some particular god, Frey, Thor, etc. The joint office was usually hereditary. In the *Eyrbyggia Saga* Rolf, called Thorolf because he was a great friend of Thor, both in Norway and later in Iceland where he settled, raised a temple in Iceland of which he was *góthi*. His son Stein was dedicated by him to Thor, and hence called Thorstein. His son Grim was in turn given to Thor and now called Thorgrim, becoming *góthi* in turn.

There is some evidence that certain women had priestly functions, perhaps a near relation of the *góthi*, and occasionally acting for him. Such a woman was called *gydja* and might even own a temple. The god Frey had a young priestess in his temple, regarded as his consort, and who went round yearly among the people with his sacred car. There were also prophetesses or divineresses among the Germanic peoples, as Tacitus shows, held in veneration. One of these, Veleda, among the Bructeri, was regarded with great respect, especially for foretelling the destruction of the Roman host. She lived in seclusion, that people might hold her in greater awe, a relative communicating between her and those who consulted her. She was regarded almost as a divinity. Such women, *spåkonur*, *völur*, wise-women, had a considerable place among the Scandinavians. At their lowest they were witches, but in their higher aspect much honour was paid to them. The *Voluspa*, that great poem which tells of the Doom of the gods, is a long recital made by a *völva* who has here a supernatural character, for she seems to be of the kin of the giants, who had fed her in past days, and she has also a comprehensive knowledge of past and future. Odin called her up, possibly from the dead, and forced her to answer his questions, for which she received his reward. She recognized him for what he was and revealed secrets of his own to him. The actual *völur* were believed to possess hidden knowledge as soothsayers and dealers in magic. Such spæwives went round to houses and were well received and feasted, a high seat being prepared for them, in the hope that they would give a hopeful destiny to the children of the house. Sometimes they were said to consult spirits about the future, which they foretold when enquiries were made of them.

CHAPTER VII

MAGIC AND DIVINATION

THE practice of divination is described by Tacitus as it existed among the Germanic tribes. Parts of a twig were marked with signs and thrown on a white cloth. Then the priest, if it were a public matter, or the head of a family if private, invoked the gods and took up the pieces to the number of three and interpreted the signs. If they proved favourable, the result was accepted. If not, the process was repeated on another day. Divination from the flight and cries of birds was also used, as well as from the neighing of white horses, kept in a sacred grove, at the time of their being yoked to a consecrated chariot, which was accompanied by the priest and king. The horses were supposed to know the divine will.

The first method was used by the Scandinavians, the slips of wood being marked with certain signs, each having a different meaning, or, as at a later period, by runes. The casting of these to obtain knowledge of a future event was used. The origin of runes was ascribed to Odin, who arranged runes and wrote them, as is said in *Sigrdrifumal*. Another stanza of the same poem speaks of them as carved on wood, then shaved off and mixed with the sacred mead, a mythical account of their invention and use. The same poem gives a list of runes which it is good to know, to be written on the sword-hilt for success, on the palm of the hand to ensure an easy childbirth, on oars or the rudder to give safety at sea, and the like. The value of the runes depended on the secret knowledge of their meaning. *Vigaglum's Saga* speaks of marks or runes engraved on sword or spear.

Magic songs or charms were also used. A list of these is given in the Eddic poem *Havamal*, for help in sickness, for use of leechcraft, for blunting an enemy's sword, for breaking fetters, for stopping the flight of an arrow, for averting the harm intended by one who sent a root on which runes were

carved, to quench fire, to neutralize hatred, to calm the waves
in a storm, to avert the power of night-riders or witches, and
others. These were perhaps akin to the formula in the Merseburg
charm, by which the healing of a lamed animal was effected
by repeating the story which told how some of the gods
healed Balder's horse. A charm of this kind is ancient and
widespread.

The Scandinavians also drew omens from the flight or
cry of birds, a raven croaking was believed to presage a king's
death. Those who left Norway to settle elsewhere offered
sacrifice for guidance, and in one account three ravens were
hallowed to show the way to the voyagers, who let each fly
off from the ship. Two came back to it, the third flew in the
direction where a landing was found. In Scandinavia also at
one sacred grove horses were kept for divination by neighing.
How this was interpreted is unknown, but great importance
was attached to the result.

Magic (*seidr*) was much practised for beneficial or harmful
purposes both by men and women. Odin himself was taunted
by Loki in the Eddic poem *Lokasenna* with having used spells
and charms like witches, himself disguised as a witch, and in
the *Ynglinga Saga* he is described as a master of magic, a
teacher of spells and charms. He is also called father of magic
in another poem. The *Hyndluljod* speaks of the *völur*, female
magicians or wise-women, and of the *vitkar* or *seidberendr*,
male wizards, giving them a fictitious ancestry. Of these the
völur are of greater importance. Odin went to Hel and there
he came to a *völva's* grave and by magic raised her up to tell
the meaning of Balder's dream. Spells were spoken over things
on which runes were carved with the intention of causing
harm. Other spells were for a better purpose, e.g., those
spoken during a famine by a woman caused every sound to be
full of herring.

A more demoniac aspect of magic was practised by the
trollkona, *kveldrida*, or *myrkrida*, who rode by night, sometimes
on a wolf bridled with snakes. They could change their forms,
and cause disease or death or storms. An example of the last
occurs in the *Eyrbyggia Saga* where Thorod bargained with
Thorgrim to raise a storm against Biorn. There came then

fog, rain, snow, hail, and darkness. There were actual witches, besides these more or less mythical night-riders, but they could be overcome by charms. For the harm which they did actual witches might be summoned to a moot or even stoned to death.

CHAPTER VIII

THE SCANDINAVIAN UNIVERSE

FOR the Scandinavian view of creation, taken from the Prose Edda which uses earlier poetic writings, we begin with a kind of chaos called Ginnunga-gap. Part of it faced north towards Niflheim, the region of mist and cold, whence flowed into it icy streams from the well Hvergelmir, forming ice. South of Ginnunga-gap was Muspell, a hot region, from which flowed out glowing masses. These melted the ice, forming a kind of yeast, and out of this came the giant Ymir. From him came the race of Frost-giants. For awhile he slept, sweat broke out from him, and a male and female grew under his left hand. One of his feet begat a six-headed son with the other. These were the first Frost-giants. From the dripping rime sprang a cow named Audumla, from whose udders flowed streams of milk by which Ymir was fed. Audumla was nourished by licking the salty blocks of ice. By her licking these, was produced first hair, next day a head, finally a whole being named Buri, fair, great and mighty. His son was Borr, whose wife was Bestla, daughter of the giant Bolthorn. Their sons were Odin, Vili, and Ve. These three slew Ymir, and so much blood flowed from him that the race of the Frost-giants was drowned, except Bergelmir who escaped with his household in a ship. From him came a new race of Frost-giants.

Now Odin, Vili, and Ve drew the body of Ymir into the middle of Ginnunga-gap, and from his flesh was formed the earth, from his blood the sea, from his bones the rocks, from his teeth gravel and stones. The sea was like a ring about the earth. Of Ymir's skull was formed the sky, stretching above the four corners of the earth. At each corner was set a dwarf. From the sparks out of Muspellheim were made the lights in the sky and above it, to illumine heaven and earth. Of these were sun, moon, and stars. Some of these lights wandered free, to the others were given their courses.

The earth was round and flat, ringed by the deep sea.

Along its edge were given lands for the giants to inhabit. In the centre of the earth was raised a citadel of defence against the giants. For it the brows of Ymir were used and it was called Midgard, or Middle-earth, for human habitation. Of Ymir's brain thrown into the air were formed the clouds. Trees were made from his hair.

This account from the Prose Edda is fairly consistent, though it leaves some things unexplained, but it is in keeping with creation myths found elsewhere. But there is another version of creation which seems to regard the earth not as made of Ymir's body, but raised out of the sea by Odin, Vili, and Ve. Again such a myth, briefly referred to in *Voluspa*, is not unknown elsewhere.

The Prose Edda continues by telling how the three gods were walking by the sea when they found two trees, out of which they made the parents of the human race. They gave them spirit and life, wit and feeling, form, speech, hearing and sight. Their dwelling was in Midgard, and their names were Askr and Embla. Of this creation of man and woman there is a variant in the poem *Voluspa*. Here Odin, Hœnir, and Lodr find Askr and Embla without life. Odin gave them soul, Hœnir reason, Lodr heat. Lodr appears to be another name of Loki.

The gods then made for themselves the city called Asgard or Troy, an interpretation of Asgard due to the conception of the gods as earlier kings and heroes with Troy as their dwelling. One of Odin's abodes is Hlidskjolf, where from his high seat he surveys all lands. The Prose Edda goes on to say that from Odin and his consort Frigg (whence she came is not explained) sprang the Æsir.

The heavenly Asgard has a great house or hall called Gladsheim, all of gold, with seats for the gods. Another house for the goddesses was called Vingolf.

The creation of the dwarfs is then described. The gods remembered that these had come alive in the earth or underneath it, like maggots in flesh, viz., the flesh of Ymir. Now these receive human form and understanding. They still live in the earth and in stones. The *Voluspa* account differs slightly from this. They were formed out of the bones and flesh of the giants Brimir and Blain. Many names of dwarfs are given, Móllsognir the first, Durinn the second, and these in turn created many dwarfs in human form.

How far this myth of creation was known among all Scandinavian people or among the Teutons generally is unknown. No creation myth of the latter has survived. The only possible point of contact is what Tacitus says, that from the sacred salt springs near the Saale, salt was obtained by evaporating the water on a pile of burning wood, the different elements of fire and water thus producing salt. This actual practice has a certain resemblance to the myth of the origin of Ymir.

Besides the general home of the gods some of them had a separate dwelling. Thus Valhall in Gladsheim, most beautiful of places, is Odin's heaven of warriors. Valaskjolf is also his abode, in which is Hlidskjolf with his high seat. In heaven is also Gimle, fairest of all, the future abode of the righteous. The hall of Heimdall, Himinbjorg, is at the heaven end of the bridge Bifrost. Thor's place is Thruthheim, with its great hall Bilskirnir. Breithablik was Balder's abode; Glitnir, roofed with silver and pillared with gold, that of his son Forseti, Alfheim that of Frey and the *alfar*. Below heaven was Midgard, the abode of men. Around its edge were mountains, the place of the giants, Jötunheim. Connecting heaven and earth was the bridge Bifrost, the rainbow, of three colours, strong, made with cunning and magic. On it Heimdall keeps watch to prevent the giants making their way into heaven. Each day the gods ride over it to the tree Yggdrasil to give dooms. This brings us to consideration of this tree, variously conceived, but mainly regarded as a world-tree. Two points may be noticed. First, what has already been said of the *irminsul* among the Saxons, a huge tree, a "universal column," sustaining all things, or the symbol of such a mythical tree. Such actual or mythical trees were often supposed to support the sky. Second, beside houses there was often a tree planted when the house was built, the *vårdträd*, as it was called in Sweden, which guarded the house and was looked upon as sacred. A similar tree, with far-spreading branches ever green, its origin known to no one, stood beside the temple at Uppsala. Yggdrasil may at first have been a kind of *vårdträd* standing beside Odni's hall or Valhall, the grove or tree Glasir, its leaves of gold, fairest of all trees. Such a tree might be developed into a world-tree, like the symbolic *irminsul*. Different pictures of Yggdrasil are given in the Eddic poems, and Snorri, using these, gives another which seems to be mistaken on one point in that he places one of the three great roots of the tree in heaven. In *Voluspa* a world-tree has nine divisions, symbolizing the nine worlds. Later in the poem this tree is called Yggdrasil. It is watered with the healing water from Urd's well where dwell the three Norns, and thence come the dews that fall in the valleys. Under the tree is Heimdall's horn, the Gjallarhorn. The poem *Svipdagsmal* speaks of the tree as Mimameith, Mimir's tree, which branches out over all lands. None knows whence are its roots. Under it is Mimir's well, and on its top the cock Vithofnir, glittering like gold, which keeps watch over the enemies of the gods. In another poem the tree is apparently referred to as Hoddmimir's wood, in which a human pair are hidden from the catastrophe which ends all things.

Three roots of this tree are spoken of in the poem *Grimnismal*, one extends to Hel, under another are the Frost-giants, under the third the lands of men. An eagle sits at the top of the tree, and the squirrel Ratatosk runs up and down the tree, reporting the words of the eagle to the dragon Nidhogg far beneath. The upper branches are nibbled by a hart, or by four of these. The dragon Nidhogg, or many serpents, gnaw the roots of the tree.

The Prose Edda is confusing in its account of the tree, putting one of its roots in heaven. Of the two others, one is among the Frost-giants, the other over Niflheim or Hel. Beneath the third is the spring Hvergelmir, whence flow many rivers. Yggdrasil is the greatest of all trees, its branches spread over all the world, even over heaven. At the root which goes down to the Frost-giants is Mimir's well. At the third root is the well of Urd, one of the Norns. To this place the gods ride daily over Bifrost to hold their tribunal. The Norns draw water from this well each day, mingling it with the clay which lies about the tree, which they sprinkle with this to prevent its withering or rotting.

Immediately before describing the ash Yggdrasil the poem *Grimnismal* speaks of a tree Laerad which stands by Odin's hall, on the branches of which the hart Eikthyrnir feeds, and from his horns a stream falls into Hvergelmir. The she-goat Heidrun also bites its branches, and each day fills the pitchers with mead from her udders. This is so copious, as Snorri says, that the Einherjar or champions become drunk with it. Presumably this tree is identical with the ash Yggdrasil, but it may be another picture of it differing from that which follows. Some critics have regarded it as representing the upper part of Yggdrasil.

All that is said of the tree makes it difficult to obtain a very clear conception of it. But as far as that is possible the idea of such a world-tree is grand, and though in other mythologies such trees occur, none of these quite approach the picture of it presented to our minds, even if that is not quite complete or harmonious in its parts. The tree also comes into the great myth of the Doom of the gods which tells how then it trembles and shakes in sympathy with the fear which pervades heaven and earth. Carlyle saw in it an emblem of the Present which holds in it Past and Future, the tree "has its roots deep down in the Death-kingdoms, among the oldest dead dust of men, and with its boughs reaches always beyond the stars, and in all times and places is one and the same Life-tree."

CHAPTER IX

THE FUTURE LIFE

THE Scandinavians held the dead in reverence, their burial-places, barrows or graves, were sacred, and sacrifice was made at them. These barrows or graves were the abode of the dead, as their houses were of the living, and a common phrase was that so-and-so had "died into the hill." The barrow might be an artificial mound, failing that burial in a hill was used. An example of the latter occurs in the *Eyrbyggia Saga.* Thorolf, an early settler in Iceland, selected a hill on Thorsness called Holy-fell as a place of burial for himself and his kindred. It was so sacred that no unwashed person was to look upon it, no man or beast was to be slain on it. In it the dead were believed to be alive, and one evening the fell was seen open on one side. Fires blazed in it. Clamour was heard and the clash of drinking vessels. Words of welcome were heard spoken to Thorstein, son of Thorolf, and his crew, and it was soon after heard that these were drowned. Aud, a Christian woman, set up crosses at certain hillocks. Her kinsmen, heathen, held them holy, and a barrow was made there and sacrifices offered. They believed that they would die into the hillocks. Asmund was laid in a ship, within a mound, and his thrall, who had slain himself, was placed in the ship. Asmund's wife dreamed that he told her that the thrall annoyed him. The howe was opened and the thrall buried elsewhere. That the dead are alive in their barrows is illustrated from one story, that of Thorsten Oxfoot, in which they fight each other, but, as in the Valhall belief, the wounds which they give each other are healed next moment. These howes were not to be profaned. On that of Aswolf a cow-girl was wont to wipe her feet. She dreamt that he appeared to her and warned her not to do this.

Barrows were generally near homesteads, as Icelandic evidence proves. Important matters were discussed upon them, the results were then supposed to be favourable. Generally the dead were helpful to their descendants, especially when due reverence was paid to them, one form of which was a feast in their honour and the drinking of toasts to their memory. Enquiry about the future was sometimes made of them, or they were consulted on important matters or their aid was sought. In the *Svipdagsmal*, Svipdag went to the mound of his mother Groa, "the mound of death," to get her help in his search for Menglod. This she gives him by communicating to him a number of runes. She ends by saying that she has stood at the door or entrance of the mound in speech with him. A further illustration of this is given in the *Harbardsljoth* when Harbard, who is Odin in disguise, speaks of learning his words from the old dead who dwell in their barrows.

Besides this family cult of the dead at their barrows, there is evidence for a cult of kings and heroes after their deaths. Or, again, the belief that it was fortunate to have the body of a king buried in the land. When Halfdan the Black died, who had been much honoured, there was much competition for his body, the belief being that wherever it was buried plenty would follow in that place. So it was divided into four and each part laid in a mound in four places.

The dead sometimes made themselves known to the living through dreams, as Asmund did to Thora, or as a king buried in his barrow did to a man who had praised him highly, telling him to look for treasure buried in it.

One aspect of the dead being alive in their barrows was of a harmful kind, usually when they had been of evil life. In stories about these, they are much more substantial than ghosts. Thorolf Halt-foot was buried in a howe. Cattle which went near it became mad and died. A herdsman was found with all his bones broken. Thorolf was seen at his former home, and his hauntings caused his wife's death. He was taken from his howe and buried in a remote place. But later his hauntings were resumed, and men and cattle were slain. Now his burial-place was again opened, his body burned, and the ashes cast into the sea. In the *Grettis Saga* Karr from his barrow does much harm, until Grettir opened it, fought Karr, and took much treasure from it. He had cut off Karr's head and laid it at his thigh, thus preventing him doing more harm. In the same Saga Glam killed men and animals. He rode on house-roofs

and caused great terror. Grettir wrestled and fought with him
in the house which he had come to haunt, and after a long and
fierce struggle, struck off Glam's head and placed it by his
thigh. Then the body was burned and the ashes buried deep
in the ground.

The name *haug-bui*, "barrow-wight," was used for
such terrifying beings, as bodily and as vital after death as
before it.

It is possible that, as in Celtic religion, the belief in a
barrow or group of barrows or a hill being the dwelling of the
dead gave place to the idea of a subterranean place of the dead,
such as the Hel of Eddic belief. How early such a belief began
is not known, nor yet how soon the idea of Valhall as a special
abode for dead warriors arose. It is noticeable, too, that while
"dying into the hill" is often spoken of in the Sagas, the belief
in Hel hardly occurs, if at all, in these. But that it is possible
to hold at one time differing conceptions of life after death can
be illustrated from many religions. An excellent example of
this occurs in *Helgakvitha Hundingsbana* in the Poetic Edda.
Helgi died and was received into Valhall, but a howe was
made in his memory, and presumably his body was buried
in it. For we are told then that one of his wife Sigrun's maidens
saw him ride to the hill with many men. She told Sigrun, who
went to the mound and spoke with Helgi. He was wet and
cold, and he told her that this was because of her tears. She
slept in his arms, and then he said that he must ride away to
Valhall ere the cock wakes the warriors. Next night Sigrun
went to the mound again, in hope that he would return from
Odin's seat. A double existence in the mound and in Valhall
is implied.

The references to the subterranean Hel in the Eddas are
somewhat contradictory. Thus Snorri says that evil men go to
Hel and thence down to Niflhel which is in the ninth world.
Again he tells how Hel, Loki's monstrous daughter, was cast
by Odin into Niflheim with power over nine worlds to apportion
abodes to all who were sent to her, those who died in sickness
and old age. This seems to be a narrowing of the conception of
Hel as an abode of all the dead, perhaps due to the idea of
Valhall as a place for dead warriors. In this second passage

nothing is said of the dead who go to Hel being wicked. Possibly Snorri misunderstood his sources. Loki's monstrous daughter, who rules Hel, is a personification of that place. She is described in repellent terms, but is not always clearly distinguished from the realm of Hel. To it Balder came after his death, not to Valhall as might be expected. When he and his steed were consumed on the pyre he rode to Hel by the Hel-way. As a result of Balder's evil dreams before his death, Odin in disguise rode on Sleipnir down to Niflhel to consult a dead *völva* about these. First he encountered the hound Garm, guardian of the approach to Hel. Then he entered Hel and came to the *völva's* grave and, raising her up, compelled her to answer his questions. Why she is buried in Hel and not on earth is not explained. It is clear from her answers what Hel was supposed to be. There are benches and platforms decked with gold, and mead is brewed for Balder. After Balder's death Hermodr rode to Hel to try to win him thence. Nine days and nights he rode through deep dales and reached the river Gjöll, crossing it by a bridge thatched with gold. The bridge is guarded by the maiden Modgudr. She asked his name, and said that on the previous day five companies of dead men had ridden over the bridge, yet the bridge thunders no less under this solitary rider who looks not like a dead man. Then he tells her why he has come and learns that Balder had ridden over the Hel-way. Hermodr reached the gate of Hel and leaped his steed over it. In the hall he saw Balder sitting in the high seat. Next morning he begged Hel to let Balder go, but she said that this could not be unless everything wept for him. Hermodr returned from Hel. Nanna, Balder's wife, who had died of grief for him, was in Hel, and sent Fulla a golden ring, and to Frigg a linen smock and other gifts, while Balder sent to Odin his ring Draupnir, which had been placed on his pyre, for a remembrance. In neither of these descriptions does Hel seem to be a place of gloom, like the Greek Hades or the Hebrew Sheol. The poem *Helreid Brynhildar* tells how Brynhild was burned in her chariot on a pyre and went in it to Hel. Though a Valkyrie she does not go to Valhall. But in a late Saxon poem Hel seems to be the place of warriors, for after a battle between Saxons and Franks, the poet asks,

"Where could there be an *infernus* (here equivalent to Hel) to contain such a multitude of the slain?"

The hall of Hel has many benches, and there the dead sit; they eat, they drink mead. They did not always travel the Helway alone. Sometimes servants slain with them attended them. They were provided with shoes, the *Hel-sko*, tied on their feet for the journey.

Valhall, "Hall of the slain," as the future abode of the dead warriors, may have been developed or extended in the Viking age, and with the worship of Odin. Valhall was established as a place for all who should fall in battle, Odin's wish-sons or adopted sons, the champions (*einherjar*), the way to it being called "the way of the slain." Hence Odin was called Valfather, "father of the slain," for all who fell in fight were his. By their means the gods were to be helped when the time of their Doom arrived. Multitudes of warriors will be there, yet not enough for the last conflict. Valhall is a vast hall in Odin's favourite abode, Gladsheim. It is of great height and is roofed with golden shields. Spears are its rafters; swords give light in it; its benches are strewn with breastplates. This enormous hall has five hundred and forty doors, through each of which will go eight hundred warriors, yet it is never crowded.

According to the *Ynglinga Saga*, Odin himself had ordained that men should be cremated with their goods, for with such wealth as a man had would he then come to Valhall. In actual custom horses and chariots were consumed on the pyre of warriors, so that they rode or drove to Valhall.

The warriors are fed on the flesh of the boar Sæhrimnir, cooked in a vast kettle by Andhrimnir, the cook of the gods. There is always enough of it to feed the great multitude. The boar is whole again in the evening, ready to be cooked again next morning. The goat Heidrun which stands by the hall feeds on the branches of Laerad (p. 157). Her udders become filled with mead, filling a vast tun, and this suffices for the drink of the champions, so much so that they become intoxicated. They are served with this mead.

The sport of the champions is to don their armour and fight each other daily in the court. They fell each other, but their wounds heal, they return to life, and sit down to their banquet. This conception of the daily fight of the warriors is illustrated from the story told by Snorri of King Hedinn and King Hogni and their forces in the battle called "the Hjadnings' Fight," waged on account of Hild, carried off by Hedinn. They fought all day and by night went to their ships. By magic Hild revived the slain, and when the battle was renewed next day, the revived dead fought also. This now goes on continually. The slain, their weapons and shields, are turned to stone, but at dawn become as they had been. This will continue till the Doom of the gods.

It is obvious that in the Valhall belief the warriors are something more bodily than souls.

"Being guest in Valhall," "going to Odin," were phrases for death. The Valkyries were sent out by Odin to choose the slain from the battlefield. They rode out as to war, they gave victory, they led the fallen to Valhall. Sometimes Odin himself was represented as taking part in battles, and there choosing or even slaying those whom he desired.

The belief in Valhall, in the prospect of being with Odin as his champions, must have furnished men with bravery and endurance in fight, though it cannot be said to be an ideal conception of a future life, even if it illustrates a certain aspect of Scandinavian life, that of the warrior.

CHAPTER X

THE FATE OF THE GODS AND OF THE WORLD

IN some passages of the Eddas there is reference to a dark fate in store for the deities, for heaven and earth. It is called the Doom or Weird of the gods. This fate, from which there could be no escape, had its beginnings in the far past.

In their golden age the gods lived in Idavoll, but that age ended with the coming of three giant maids from Jötunheim, possibly the Norns, who are said to be of the giants' kin. If so, the meaning would seem to be that the gods themselves were now subject to the power of fate. Another precursor of the end was the war with the Vanir, the cause of which, according to *Voluspa*, was the gods' ill-treatment of one of them, Gollveig, whom they put to death more than once, for she always returned to life. Then the gods' habitation was broken down, and a giant artificer was employed to restore it within a certain time, his condition being that he should then receive Freyja and the sun and moon. Through Loki's stratagem the work was not completed within the stipulated time. Giant-fury possessed the artificer, but Thor slew him with his hammer. Thus, as *Voluspa* says, the oaths and pledges of the gods were broken. They are said to have perceived from prophecy that they would have great misfortunes, e.g., from Loki's brood, the Midgard serpent, Hel, and the Fenris wolf, all of whom they meanwhile overcame. Loki caused the death of Balder, another event of evil omen for the gods, though Loki himself was bound.

Preceding the end, according to Snorri, comes the Fimbul winter, lasting three years without intervening summers, with terrible frost, snow, and wind, and accompanied by battles and a general relaxing of morality among men. Some of the poems speak of the sinking of the earth into the sea, the sea seeking heaven itself as it flows over the earth. One wolf, born of a Troll-woman, swallows the sun, which he has always pursued;

another, also of her brood, swallows the moon. These are eclipse-myths which have found their way into this picture of the Doom. The stars also vanish from the heavens.

Earth trembles, trees are torn up, rocks are broken. The dwarfs roar by their stone doors. The Fenris wolf breaks loose from its bonds; the sea flows over the land because the Midgard serpent is stirring and rising over the earth. The ship Naglfar, made of the nails of dead men, which should have been cut before their burial, floats, steered by the giant Hrymr. Garm, the monstrous watch-dog of the gate of Hel, howls aloud. The Fenris wolf advances with gaping mouth, one jaw reaching to heaven, one to earth, fire bursting from nostrils and mouth. The Midgard serpent blows forth venom. The sons of Muspell, the region of fire, led by the giant Surtr, ride forth, fire burning before and after them. They pass over Bifrost bridge, which now breaks. Then they go to the field called Vigridr, measuring a hundred miles in each direction, where the final battle is to be fought. Here, too, come the Fenris wolf, the Midgard serpent, Hrymr, and the Frost-giants. The champions of Hel, headed by Loki, come in a ship.

Meanwhile Heimdall rises and blows his horn to waken the gods, who take counsel together. Odin rides to Mimir's well to seek advice from Mimir's head. The ash Yggdrasil trembles. Terror spreads over heaven and earth. The gods don their armour and ride to Vigridr, Odin preceding them with his helmet and spear, and the champions from Valhall follow. He joins battle with the Fenris wolf. Thor is beside him, but can be of no help, for he is attacked by the Midgard serpent. Frey has a mighty fight with Surtr, but he falls, for he had given his magic sword which fought of itself, to Skirnir. The monstrous dog Garm is freed and fights with Tyr, each slaying the other. Thor slays the Midgard serpent, but venom blown at him by the dying monster causes his death. The wolf swallows Odin, but Vidarr, the strong god, sets one foot on its lower jaw, and seizing the upper jaw, tears out its gullet. On the foot set on the jaw he wears the shoe which the scraps of leather cut from all men's shoes at the toe and heel have helped to make (therefore, says Snorri, all who would help the gods should throw these away), Loki and Heimdall fight and each slays the other. Finally Surtr casts fire over the earth and burns it up.

Nothing is said of the conduct or fate of the champions from Valhall, a large company, for in the poem *Grimnismal*, it has five hundred doors, through each of which go eight hundred champions to the last fight, when they go forth to war with the wolf. Nor is anything said of the fate of the giants. But presumably all perish. The references to the formation of the ship Naglfar out of dead men's nails, and to Vidarr's shoe from scraps of leather, point, especially the former, to the long age supposed to elapse before the final catastrophe.

But this impressive event, so wonderfully told both by Snorri and by the *Voluspa* poet, is not the end, or rather it is an end to the existing order to be followed by a new beginning. The gods are dead, earth and men have perished. Does nothing else follow? Will the dead not have immortal life? The answer is that there will be a future world with many good abodes and many evil, as Snorri says. Best of all, fairest of all, will be the hall on Gimle, thatched with gold, which even before the end, stands at the south end of heaven, and survives the destruction of heaven and earth. It is for the good and righteous who will enjoy endless delight. The *Voluspa* has a passage which refers to retribution after death for adulterers, murderers, and the treacherous in Nastrand, an evil place, woven of snakes, whose heads drop venom into it. Streams are formed of this in which these evil ones wade, and the dragon Nidhogg sucks the blood of the slain. Snorri seems to connect this with the new world, but the *Voluspa* poet does not do so. But here we may see the partial influence of Christian beliefs about the future.

There is to be a new earth emerging out of the sea, green and fair, where fruits and harvests will spring forth of themselves. The gods meet in Idavoll and talk of the Midgard serpent; they recall the past, and Odin's mighty runes. The golden tables stand once more in the grass, once owned by the gods. But who are the gods who appear here? Vidarr and Vali, sons of Odin, who survive the fire of Surtr; Mothi and Magni, sons of Thor, who inherit his hammer; the sons of Vili and Ve; Balder and Hodr come back from Hel; and Hœnir, who now has the gift óf prophecy. They sit and talk of old times. The other gods have perished.

It may seem strange that, even in a polytheistic religion, gods should perish. On the other hand it must be remembered that they are not naturally eternal. They came into existence at a given time; giants had existed before them and from them some of them had sprung. Their continued existence depended upon their eating Idunn's apples, whenever they felt themselves growing old: then they became young once more, "So will it be even to the Doom of the gods," said Snorri.

Two of mankind, Lif and Lifthrasir, have been hidden in Hoddmimir's wood and survive the doom and the fire of Surtr. They are the parents of the new race of mankind, and feed on the morning dews. A new sun shines over the earth, daughter of her that was swallowed by the wolf.

Then both the *Voluspa* and the short *Voluspa* poem included in the *Hyndluljoth* tell of a Mighty One, greater than all, his name not to be spoken, who will rule all lands and hold all power.

In this strange account of the end of the gods, the main point is that they are opposed by monstrous evil powers and giants who overcome them and themselves perish. Here is dualism, but not a moral dualism, it is not a contest between good and evil. It is not easy to assign a reason for this conflict, though it had its origin in the far past. The *Voluspa* doubtless incorporates earlier myths, but though it was composed in a time when Christianity was about to overthrow the old paganism and though the poet may have known important Christian doctrines and possibly have been influenced by them, the poem itself deals with pagan beliefs and myths. Even the reference to the "Mighty One" yet to come, in which a reference to Christ has been seen by some, is not necessarily derived from Christianity. The conception of Gimle, the abode of the righteous, and of the dreadful place of punishment for certain sinners, need not have been adopted from Christian sources. Most religions have some kind of Paradise for the good or brave, and some kind of Tartarus for obnoxious people. The *Voluspa* poet, whether this place of punishment was to exist after the Doom or not, was using an old belief that certain crimes most abhorred among his race would be punished beyond the grave. The destruction of the world by fire is a myth found elsewhere, in Indian belief, in Greece, among the Celts.

The conception of the two human beings, Lif and Lifthrasir, hid in Mimir's grove, has a certain parallel in the ancient Persian belief about Yima's *vara* or enclosure, prepared against the coming of terrible winters, where a human pair appear, by whom others are begotten, and live happy lives. There are also medieval tales, possibly based on much earlier myths, about a place called Gudmund's realm or Odainsakar or Land of Living Men—*Jörd lifanda manna*, where the dwellers are not the dead, and where beauty and happiness prevail.

SUGGESTED BOOKS FOR FURTHER STUDY

CELTIC

Prof. E. Anwyl, *Celtic Religion in pre-Christian Times*, 1906. A brief but interesting account (68 pp.) of the subject.

G. Dottin, *Manuel pour servir a l'étude de l'antiquité celtique*. 2e ed. 1915 (revised and augmented, an excellent and useful study).

C. I. Elton, *Origins of English History*, 1890. Interesting for its discussion of Celtic affairs.

P. W. Joyce, *Old Celtic Romances*, 2nd ed., 1894, gives some of the Irish tales referred to in this book.

A. Nutt and K. Meyer, *The Voyage of Bran*, 2 vols., 1895–97, a comprehensive study of the Irish Elysium or Wonderland and its people.

Sir John Rhys, *Celtic Britain*, 4th ed., 1908. *Celtic Folk-Lore*, 2 vols., 1891, a valuable survey. *Hibbert Lectures on Celtic Heathendom*, 1888.

J. A. MacCulloch, *Celtic Mythology*, in "The Mythology of all Races" series, 1918, deals mainly with the myths in old Irish and Welsh literatures, giving full summaries of these. *The Religion of the Ancient Celts*, 1911, a comprehensive study of the religion in all its aspects.

SCANDINAVIAN

H. M. Chadwick, *The Cult of Othin*, 1899.

W. A. Craigie, *The Religion of Ancient Scandinavia*, short but useful study. *Scandinavian Folk-Lore*, 1896, selections and translations. *The Icelandic Sagas*, 1913, a valuable introduction.

Edda, The Poetic, translated with an Introduction and Notes, by Henry Adams Bellows, 2 vols. in 1, 1923.

Edda, The Prose, by Snorri Sturluson. Translated with an Introduction by A. G. Brodeur, Ph.D., 1916.

There are other editions of the Eddas, but these will be found most useful.

G. Vigfusson and F. Y. Powell, *Corpus Poeticum Boreale*, 2 vols, 1883. Contains most of the early poetry. *Origines Islandicæ*, sagas and native writings relating to the settlement and early history of Iceland, 2 vols., 1905, contains many notices of the religion.

The Saga Library, edited by W. Morris and E. Magnusson, 6 vols., 1891–1905, contains the most important sagas, with valuable notes and introductions.

The Story of Burnt Njal, from the Njal's Saga, by G. W. Dasent, 2 vols., 1861.

The Grettis Saga, translated by E. Magnusson and W. Morris, 1869.

Saxo Grammaticus, Gesta Danorum. The first five books, translated by C. Elton, Notes etc., by F. York Powell, 1894.

J. A. MacCulloch, *Eddic Mythology*, in "The Mythology of all Races" series, 1930, gives a full account of all aspects of Scandinavian Mythology, with surveys of all the myths in the Eddas.

INDEX

CELTIC

A

Abnoba, 14, 30
Aife, 48
Altars, 64f.
Amairgen, 83
Ambicatus, 9
Amulets, 78
Ancestor worship, 84
Andarta, 31
Andrasta, 30, 31, 56, 63
Anglesey, a Druidic stronghold, 56
Animals, 17f.
Annwfn, 32, 34, 36, 90
Anu, 42
Apollo, 24, 25, 31, 86
Apollonius, 86
Arawn, 34
Arduinna, 14
Arianrhod, 34f.
Artaios, 18, 37
Artemis, 18, 53, 54
Arthur, 87, 91
Artificers, divine, 44
Artio, 18
Artogenos, 22
Auguries, 55f.
Avagddu, 36
Avallon, 90

B

Badb, 23, 42, 43, 87
Badbcatha, 43
Balor, 41
Bards, 73f.
Bear, 18
Becuma, 94
Belatucadros, 26, 31
Belenos, 17, 25, 31, 59
Belgae, 11
Beli, 31, 34, 35
Belisama, 27
Beltane, 17, 58, 60
Bile (sacred tree), 14
Blodeuwedd, 35
Boand, 43

Boar, 17f.
Bodb, 48
Bodb Dearg, 43
Bodua, 43
Bonfires, sacred, 59
Bormanus, 26
Boimo, Borvo, 25, 26, 64
Boudicca (Boadicea), 56
Braciaca, 26
Bran, 32f.
Bran, head of, 33, 57
Bran, in Irish story, 92
Branwen, 32f.
Brendan, St., 92
Bres, 40f.
Brian, 41
Bricrui's Feast, 48
Brigantia, 31, 42
Brigindu, 42
Brigit, 28, 31, 42, 43
Brigit or Bride, St., 42, 87
Brown bull of Cuailgne, 49
Brownie, 85
Brug na Boinne, 84
Brythons, 11; deities of the, 31f.

C

Cæsar, conquest of Gaul and invasion of Britain, 10; on consecrated places, 63; on division of time, 58; on Druids, 67; on deities, 25f.; on future life, 80, 81; on sacrifices, 54; on promiscuity, 93; on worship 53; his sword, 64
Caer Gwydion, 36
Caer Sidi, 36
Cairns over the dead, 85
Calendar of Coligny, 17
Camulos, 22, 31, 50
Caoilte, 50, 51
Cassiopeia, 36
Casswallawn, 34
Cathbad, 47

SCANDINAVIAN

63600